THE
MALDIVES

Kirsten Ellis, a New Zealander, is the author of a variety of travel guides. After seven years of living in Hong Kong and India, she is now based in Europe.

THE
MALDIVES

Kirsten Ellis

Photography by Dominic Sansoni

Hong Kong

Distribution in the United Kingdom, Ireland, Europe and certain Commonwealth countries by Hodder & Stoughton, Mill Road, Dunton Green, Sevenoaks, Kent TN13 2YA.

Editor: Nigel Sitwell
Series Editor: Claire Banham
Illustrations Editor: Caroline Robertson
Map Artwork: Bai Yiliang
Design: Aubrey Tse
Cover Concept: Raquel Jaramillo and Aubrey Tse
Additional photography: Gillian Ashworth 33, 156, 157

British Library in Cataloguing in Publication Data has been applied for

Production House: Twin Age Limited, Hong Kong

Printed in Hong Kong by Sing Cheong Printing Co. Ltd.

Contents

Special Topics

Maps

Excerpts

Introduction

The Maldives is one of the most attenuated countries in the world, comprising around 1,190 islands in 26 distinct coral atolls in the Indian Ocean—though no one has yet definitively counted all the islands and reeflets, even with the help of modern satellite maps. Some 200 of the islands are inhabited, 25 of them with a population of more than 1,000 people. Over 60 tourist resorts have been established among four main atolls, and are locally classified as 'uninhabited by Maldivians'. The whole country covers an area of about 93,000 square kilometres (36,000 square miles), but only a fraction of one percent of this is land, and only a small part of that is habitable.

None of this really bothers the average tourist, who only needs to know one or two things about the country—that it has the most beautiful tropical scenery, graceful coconut palms leaning over crystal-clear lagoons, coral reefs promising great snorkelling and scuba diving, and lots of sunshine.

The Maldives attracts about 200,000 tourists a year, of whom roughly a quarter are Germans, 20 percent Italians, 9 percent Japanese, 8 percent British, and a slightly smaller number of Swedes, Swiss and French. Virtually no Americans make it to these isolated islands, and very few Australians. The tourist industry began in 1972 and has consistently appealed to outdoors types, visitors who don't mind the lack of nightlife and who enjoy seclusion. Scuba divers praise the Maldives as a serious rival to the Great Barrier Reef and the Red Sea. Its transparent waters are a comfortable 27°C (81°F) all year round, and shifting currents open up fresh dive sites throughout the year.

Almost all tourists are housed in self-contained resorts, carefully distanced by the wide blue coral seas from the indigenous population. Away from the resorts, it is obvious that geographical and cultural isolation has kept the Maldives in a quirky Graham Greeneland all of its very own, a kind of Islamic paradise inbred into eccentricity and somehow barely connected to the rest of the world. In truth, convicted prisoners and international tourists share a similar fate in this paradise, for those found guilty of minor infractions of Islamic law are banished to a remote tropical island to serve a sentence of separation from their families. The tourists pay up to $250 a day for basically the same surroundings, self-exile among swaying palm trees and starched-white beaches from which, unlike their local criminal counterparts, they are free to leave after a week or two.

Each resort offers its own version of fantasy-isle accommodation ranging from the distressingly plebian to the sumptuously chic. You can be there for a few weeks without the slightest idea you're just a few degrees north of the equator and an hour from India. As sensory deprivation goes it's pretty much close to heaven, pampered amnesia with an international telephone line instead of roughing it in search of cultural exploration.

The Maldives, where nowhere is more than 15 feet above sea level, is in danger of disappearing altogether if the greenhouse effect takes hold and the ice caps melt. The capital, Malé, is still low-rise and sleepy; every time a Singapore Airlines jumbo jet thumps down on the runway at nearby Hulule airport it becomes the tallest thing in the Maldives. The capital is slow moving too. In 1988, only 440 cars were registered in all of Malé, plus 1,728 motorbikes and nearly 20,000 bicycles. The best indicator of personal wealth is the number of people making the Hajj, (the pilgrimage to Mecca every Muslim is meant to embark on once in his lifetime), which has tripled over the last four years. The one-chanel television station broadcasts to around 4,000 registered sets in the evenings, though its range extends only a few miles ouside Malé. On the positive side, the Maldives still sees no need of insurance for its car drivers, has no municipal taxes, and no personal or corporate taxation.

The society is conservative, but Maldivians are, quite rightly, quick to stress that their brand of Islam—though strictly enforced—is more pragmatic than fundamentalist. The president wields a lot of power on paper—he won more than 95 percent of the vote at his third election in 1988, in which he was the only candidate—heavily influenced by the parliament, the *Majlis*, most of whose members are elected but some of whom are appointed by the president.

The religious leaders, the *qazis*, have a major role to play, authorizing marriage contracts and serving in the courts. Early marriages are the norm at around 15 to 16 years of age for girls on outer islands and it is not uncommon for people to marry three of four times. The Maldives holds the distinction of the highest divorce rate of any United Nations-member country. In 1988, for example, there were 2,114 marriages and 1,560 divorces. Between the ages of 30 and 40 they occur in almost equal numbers, probably because it is so easy. A man merely has to voice the divorce formula three times for it to be valid, though a woman is obliged to plead her case in court.

Public decorum is enforced by nonuniformed police in Malé and tourists are advised to follow official instructions about the standard of attire expected. Women especially should wear clothing that 'must be made of material which is not see-through or diaphanous; a piece of cloth simply wrapped around the torso is not acceptable or indeed permitted,' says a government tourism leaflet.

It was not always thus. An early seventeenth-century French traveller, François Pyrard de Laval , noted that the Maldivians were an extremely lascivious people much preoccupied with sex, a characteristic that perhaps has only disappeared with tighter Islamic scrutiny. In fact, most modern visitors may find Maldivians hesitant and shy, friendly but reluctant to open up. There appear to be no words for 'please' or 'thank you' in common use, which reinforces the impression of the people being unassuming and visibly unemotional. However, the Maldivian language, known as divehi, does employ multiple levels of courtesy in addressing superiors and strangers, a bit like Japanese but not nearly so profuse. There are special forms of address for the *beyfulu*, strictly descendants of royalty and others whose ancestry is related to the Prophet, but now widened to include important families such as those of the top government leaders and foreign heads of state.

Though the Islamic courts do not impose punishments like the severing of a hand at the wrist for common thievery, the novel idea of banishment is often applied. In 1988 the courts pronounced convictions in 1,224 cases; 806 of the offenders were banished, one third of whom were women. The majority were sent away for one or two years, but two of the women were banished for life. An official survey of police court cases showed that in some years the convictions for conducting an 'illegal coital relationship' were almost a third of the figure for common theft. There's at least one penal island where the instigators of an attempted coup in 1988 are 'incarcerated' under blue skies and coconut palms. Nor is curiosity encouraged despite the country's impressive record of 95 percent literacy. In 1990, President Gayoom experimented temporarily with an open press, according to a report in the *New York Times*, only to shut down critical publications and arrest the country's best cartoonist. Young Maldivians who go abroad to study have to serve a period of 'bonded labour' on their return, a kind of national service for the intelligentsia in the sandy corridors of Maldivian bureaucracy; a one-year course overseas earns you three months, while three years overseas entails one year in government service.

Surrounded on all sides by water, the Maldives' fishing industry is its biggest revenue earner after tourism. 1988 fish exports amounted to Rf.263 million (about $27.1 million) more than triple the earnings in 1984. Just under half of that was from 19,700 tonnes of skipjack tuna which the Maldives is now advertising as having been caught using 'dolphin-friendly' methods, (ie. using a pole and long line with a single hook, net fishing being outlawed), where the crew of an eight-man boat work frantically to catch 500 fish an hour. A new line is sea cucumber, a gelatinous food delicacy praised in Chinese cuisine, exports of which went up from just Rf.220, that's just over $22, in 1985 to Rf.40 million, around $4.1 million, in 1988. The Maldives other claim to fame is that it has the world's only Coca-Cola factory that uses desalinated water. Other than that piece of unhealthy living, hypertension is unknown and with the communal life-style so well established no one in the Maldives starves.

The Maldives officially celebrated the 25th anniversary of nationhood in 1990. The changes during that time have been immense with diseases held in check, literacy made near universal, communications improved and wide-ranging social welfare programmes introduced. Foreign aid from independent agencies, development banks and foriegn governments—including generous fraternal help from other Islamic countries like Saudi Arabia—have transformed the country and the expectations of its 215,000 people, a predominantly young population expanding at a rapid 3.5 percent per year. Still, as the

Maldives displayed a GDP (Gross Domestic Product) growth rate in real terms of around 9 percent in 1989, the nation's goal of putting a telephone on every inhabited island by the year 2000 looks obtainable.

All in all, the Maldives is a fascinating country, sometimes quixotic and elusive, that deserves more exploration than a few weeks' self-imposed incarceration in a tourist resort allows. This book, I hope, will tempt you to try it.

Some Booking Agents in the UK

Maldive Travel, 3 Esher House, 11 Edith Terrace, London, SW10 0TH. Tel. 071-352-2246; fax. 071-351-3382. Run by 'The Maldive Lady', Toni de Laroque, whose personal flag of a rampant parrot flies on every island she has visited; official Maldives government representative for tourism in the UK.

Holiday Islands Ltd, 125 East Barnet Rd, New Barnet, Herts, EN4 8RF. Tel. 081-441 4064; fax. 081-449 8497.

Kuoni Travel Ltd, Kuoni House, Dorking, Surrey, RG5 4AZ. Tel. 0306–740500.

EliteVacations, 98/100 Bessborough Road, Harrow, Middlesex, HA1 3DT. Tel. 081–864 9818; fax. 081–426 9178

Thomson Worldwide, Greater London House, Hampstead Rd, London NW1 7SD. Tel. 071-387-1900.

Hayes & Jarvis. Tel. 081-748-5050.   Speedbird. Tel. 0293-611611.
Inghams. Tel. 081-780-2277.   Club Med. Tel. 071-581-1161.

General Information for Travellers

Getting There

Thanks to the tourist industry, the Maldives is well served by a host of international airlines, supplemented during the peak season (December–March) by regular charter flights, principally from Europe. Hulule International Airport near Malé is the country's only point of international entry. Colombo in Sri Lanka, Trivandrum in India, and Singapore are the main jumping-off points to reach the Maldives for independent travellers.

Scheduled airlines operating to the Maldives include Air Lanka (from Colombo), Indian Airlines (Trivandrum), PIA (Karachi), Emirates Airlines (Dubai), and Singapore Airlines (Singapore) with connections in Europe to Berlin , Zürich, Vienna, and Paris. The principal charter operators flying to the Maldives are Sterling Airways out of Stockholm, Copenhagen, Helsinki, and Athens; LTU and LTS from Düsseldorf and Munich; Balair from Zurich and Milan; Condor from Frankfurt, Munich, and Düsseldorf, Alitalia from Rome; Lauda Air from Vienna and Monarch Airways from London.

Overbooking is a recurrent problem on international flights during the peak season. It is essential to reconfirm your booking 72 hours in advance. If possible, get your booking confirmation number and a computer printout. Check-in time at the airport for international flights is two hours before scheduled take-off.

When to Go

The most pleasant time to visit the Maldives is between December and March, usually a time of endlessy sunny days and when the clear calm waters can be seen at their transparent best. However, this is the peak season so book well in advance. It should also be noted that January is the most congested month.

Weather during the low season of late April to early November is not as predictable, but prices at resorts and hotels are usually heavily discounted. The worst time to go is the time of the Southwest monsoon, between late April and late October, especially June, when there can be storms and torrential rain.

Throughout the year, temperatures range from 24°C to 33°C (75°–87°F) with a fairly high humidity level cooled by sea breezes.

Visas

Officialdom is remarkably pared down in the Maldives. Until 1978 it was one of the few countries in the world that did not require visitors to show passports on entry. Today, though, a valid passport is essential and a 30-day tourist visa is issued automatically on arrival at Hulule International Airport. Few visitors exceed this time limit, but an extension of stay can usually be granted for a further three-month period. Do this at the Department of Immigration in the Huravee Building next to the police station in Malé for a fee of Rf300. Anyone arriving without a resort booking must have at least $10 a day for their intended stay, an arbitrary limit that is quite outdated. You are expected also to have accommodation reserved, but no one checks. You can do this at the airport Tourist Information counter as you pass through immigration control.

Customs

A strict import ban is imposed on firearms, explosives, narcotic drugs and most industrial poisons or chemicals. Bear in mind that the Maldives is a strict Muslim country. In keeping with Islamic codes, it is illegal to import alcohol, pornography of any kind including nude photographs, magazines or drawings, or any idolatrous statues. Bacon, ham, or pork products also will not be welcomed. Expect to have the contents of your luggage taken out and displayed in front of a restless queue of fellow tourists by merciless customs officers, a seemingly meticulous and mandatory screening process which anyone may be subjected to, at random. Bottles of duty-free wine or spirits will be impounded by customs but can be collected when you leave. (However, drinks can be bought at the resorts.)

Bed and Airport Taxes

A tax of $6 per person per day is levied on all travellers staying in the Maldives, regardless of whether they stay in a guesthouse or resort, or cruise the blue waters. All departing travellers are required to pay an airport tax of $7. This must be paid in foreign currency, not in Maldivian rufiyas.

Time

The Maldives is five hours ahead of GMT. For comparison, it lies in the same time zone as Pakistan, is half an hour behind India and Sri Lanka, and three hours behind Singapore. Many resorts switch their own clocks one hour ahead of local time in an effort to make things less stressful when you leave to catch your flight home—which only serves to confuse if you want to listen to your favourite programme on the BBC World Service.

Climate

The Maldives straddles the equator, which puts it on a par with Kenya, Brazil and Singapore. Its climate is tropical with daytime temperatures ranging from 26°–33°C (77°–87°F) with about a three-degree drop at night under the open starry skies. There are two monsoon seasons, which are relatively mild due the country's location on the equator. The **northeast monsoon** is characterized by gentle, dry winds from November to April. It can bring some heavier rains in

September and October and heavy seas in early November. The **southwest monsoon** prevails from May to October; in April and May this brings erratic showers with higher winds later in June and July. Conditions are marginally more clement in the south than the north, with fewer storms and slightly less rainfall. Humidity is a constant 75–80 percent, which is quite bearable. Rainfall averages around 1,900 millimetres (74 inches) annually, largely during the southwest monsoon season but only picking up in August and running on sometimes through into December and even January. The water temperature is a constant 27°C (81°F) even down to a depth of 20 metres (60 feet).

Health Precautions

Any visitor arriving from areas infected with either cholera or yellow fever must be able to produce an international vaccination certificate. People coming from malaria-infected areas—especially from India and Sri Lanka—will sometimes be asked to give a blood sample, but this is usually only enforced for Indian and Sri Lanka nationals.

The vast majority of visitors to the Maldives will face no health problems, though it's wise to consult your doctor or an official vaccination centre before travelling, to check current requirements and recommendations. Vaccination against tetanus and a gamma globulin injection (against hepatitis) are advisable for all travellers. Malaria has been largely wiped out in the Maldives, but it is still advisable to take a course of antimalarial tablets. There is some evidence that long-term use of antimalarial prophylactics can be damaging to the liver and the retina, so you may wish to smother yourself with mosquito repellent, use mosquito coils, and string up a mosquito net around your bed at night instead.

The odds of falling victim to a mosquito-borne sickness—such as malaria, dengue fever, or filariasis—are quite low, especially if you spend most of your time on a resort island. The risks are greater in Malé which has the highest population density in the Maldives and hence a greater chance of transmission. Diarrhoea and stomach upsets are likely to be the only ailments you will encounter. To avoid them, take simple precautions. Drink only bottled water or water which has been boiled or sterilized. Never take a chance on the water served in Malé's cafés or water drawn from village wells. It may be wise to include some iodine solution or water purification tablets in your personal first aid kit.

If you do have an attack of diarrhoea the best way to treat it is with a diet of bland foods, such as rice, yoghurt, bananas and bread, with plenty of fluids such as weak tea to flush out your system. If problems persist more than two days, particularly if accompanied by a fever, consult a doctor as you may be suffering from dysentry, an illness that will require treatment. Emergency medical care in the Maldives is adequate and compares well with isolated parts of India. Evacuation services exist to airlift seriously ill patients away from their resorts, but you should ensure that your medical insurance covers repatriation home in case of dire emergencies. Casualty services are offered at the Central Hospital in Malé and the Swiss Flying Ambulance clinic.

Prevention is better than attempting a cure during your holiday. Increase your nonalcoholic fluid intake by three or four times, protect yourself against the sun (which will be much stronger than you're used to), and use plenty of moisturizing lotions. Don't make massive changes of diet towards fresh fruit or spicy foods. Following these simple guidelines will increase your enjoyment and resistence to illness whilst away from home.

What to Take

Light clothing is the order of the day everywhere. Remember that there are two standards, one for the almost exclusively western-inhabited resort islands and another for the sleepy Islamic capital of Malé. Wear strictly non-see-through clothes in any situation where the locals can see or bump into you. Even if you confine yourself to your resort, you would be wise to take some long-sleeved shirts and long trousers for covering up until you have got used to the sun.

Do not forget the obvious items like sun screen, a change of bathing costume, and a sunhat. Mosquito repellent, and ointment for cuts and bites, are musts. Many resorts, especially the more expensive ones, sell a wide range of beachwear, much of it very fashionable and imported. In the wet season, bring a light raincoat. A torch and spare batteries are always useful. You can buy film in Malé and the resorts but it's best to bring your own as it is cheaper that way and has probably enjoyed a better shelf life.

Money

The Maldivian unit of currency is the rufiya, abbreviated as Rf. Each 'rufe' is divided into 100 larees. Currently US$1 equals about Rf9.6. Unless otherwise stated all prices in this book are qiven in US dollars. There is no black market for the currency and visitors should change their hard currency at the airport when they arrive. Notes come in denominations of 100, 50, 20, ten, five, two and one. There is a Rf1 coin and smaller denominations of 50, 25, ten, five, two and one larees. It's worth bringing your cash in US dollars which are readily traded in the Maldives where resorts, shops and booking agents will accept the greenback in lieu of rufiyas. There are no restrictions when changing cash or travellers' cheques into rufiyas but be warned: you are only allowed to reconvert ten percent of that amount on departure, and only then if you can produce the original exchange receipts. No bank outside the Maldives will accept rufiyas.

All the major credit cards are accepted in the Maldives, although the only company to have a representative in Malé is American Express (care of Universal Enterprises, 18 Marine Drive. Tel. 32–3116/3661; fax. 32–2695).

Most resorts have their own internal systems of accounting, including chits, beads, and the like. You can settle such bills in hard currency when you leave. A package tourist can easily spend a fortnight in the Maldives and never handle a single rufiya note.

Communications

One of the marvels of the Maldives is that instantaneous international direct dialling is available from most resorts to anywhere in the world, as well as domestic links within its own scattered islands. The Maldives has one of the most sophisticated telecommunications systems in the region, installed by Dhiraagu, a joint venture between Britain's Cable and Wireless and the Maldivian government. Dhiraagu is building a high tech earth station on Villingili to replace the present one in Malé and plans to have a telephone on every island by the year 2000. Operator-connected calls come through immediately. As with hotels worldwide, resorts usually add around 10–20 percent to the cost of each call as a connection charge.

You can make telephone calls and send faxes, telexes, and cables in Malé at the Dhiraagu office, Medu Ziyaaraiy Magu, near the presidential palace, every day except Friday and Muslim holidays. Local calls in Malé can be made through rare public call boxes. Hotels and shopkeepers will lend their phone if you volunteer the Rf2 charge. Malé numbers are prefixed 32, North and South Malé Atolls by 34, Ari Atoll numbers by 35, and other islands by 34.

News From Home

English language news can be found on one page of both the two Divehi daily newspapers, *Haveeru* and *Aafathis*, but that is not much use as you can go for weeks without seeing them. TV Maldives broadcasts for five hours daily with a 20-minute English language programme at 9 pm. In fact, unless you take a short wave radio, forget about trying to keep up with the rest of the world.

Postal Services

The main post office is on the corner of Chandani Magu and Marine Drive. It keeps flexible hours not strictly related to those advertised. Officially it is open daily, except Friday, from 7.30 am–12.45 pm and from 3 pm–4.45 pm. Poste restante services are available. Overseas postcards to anywhere in the world cost Rf5 and take about ten days. As befits a small country the stamps are usually on the large size, so leave plenty of space.

Electricity

Electricity is 220-240 volts, 50 cycles AC. Plug sockets can vary widely so take an all-purpose adapter. Although the electricity supply in Malé is reasonably reliable, there is no national grid and generator-supplied power on the islands and even the capital can fluctuate. On some islands electricity is restricted to the evening hours only, so take a torch, matches, and candles.

Business Hours

Government offices are open daily, except Friday, from 7.30 am–1.30 pm. Banks are open Sunday to Thursday from 9 am–1 pm, and on Saturdays from 9–11 am. Shops in Malé open sometime between seven and eight in the morning and close between nine and 11 at night. This is feasible because Malé snoozes through a siesta period in the early afternoon, from 1.30 pm until 3 pm, and then again during the main daily prayer time from 6 pm–8 pm.

Etiquette and Understanding

English is spoken widely at a rudimentary level, a tribute to the tourist boom in the last decade and local schooling, so you will be understood both in Malé and on resort islands. However, the lack of any obvious emotion among the Maldivians is a peculiarity many Westerners may find difficult to understand. Not a great deal of fuss is ever made in greeting old friends or celebrating events such as marriages. In fact, the local language of Divehi contains no formal greeting, few expressions of concern and no words whatever for 'please' or 'thank you'. This isn't due to unfriendliness, but stems from habit and self-absorption. Unlike neighbouring India, Maldivians are not outwardly affectionate or curious. And men find it difficult to talk directly to women.

Islamic morals, however, are not to be flouted. The big taboo is physical decency. The law states absolutely 'No Nudism', the fine for which is $1,000.

Modesty is required in Malé, and may even be enforced by nonuniformed policemen eager to protect Muslim mores and local civic virtue. However, if you are sensible and bear in mind local sensibilities, you do not need to worry unduly. In general, the Maldivian attitude towards tourists is as pragmatic as that in Indonesia, and certainly not as severe as in Iran. Basically, you can do what you like in your resort, short of naked sunbathing.

Maldivians are not allowed, by law, to sell alcohol, even to tourists in hotel or resort bars. (The government imports Sri Lankans, Indian and Bangladeshis to work as bar staff.) The punishment for even this apparently mild transgression is banishment to an outer island. Do not try to look inside a mosque unless you are a practising Muslim, and never under any circumstances if you are a western woman.

The Maldivian government likes tourists but earnestly tries to keep the visitors and natives apart. The local community is very small and easily policed by gossip. If you step over the line, everyone will know about it very quickly. It's not worth it.

Tipping

Resorts and most
restaurants and cafés
in Malé add the
standard ten percent
charge for their
services. If you hire
a boat, the senior boat
boy should be tipped
at the end of the trip.
If you want to thank
anyone, most people
will appreciate a
present from the duty-
free shop, which is off-
limits for locals.
Airport baggage porters
have come to expect a
decent tip, about Rf10,
for the short walk to
the boat pier.

Shopping

Historically, the
Maldives exported
tortoiseshell, cowrie
shells, mother-of-pearl,
black coral and amber-
gris (a usually sweet
smelling, waxy substance formed in the intestines of sperm whales and used
as a fixative in perfumes). Lacquerware boxes made from wood carved on a
lathe can also be found, as can *kunnar*, leaves of the screw pine (pandanus)
made into strips, then dried and coloured. Tortoiseshell from the hawksbill
or other sea turtles is strictly prohibited either for export from the Maldives or
importation in the west, as a religious taboo and by law. Collection of turtle eggs
is not yet prohibited, but it is best to leave them where they are and not encourage their sale. That leaves stamps, T-shirts, old coins and Maldivian costumes
and sharks' jaws.

Despite the Maldives' long history as a trading outpost, there is no point in
trying to bargain in most shops. There is little to buy by way of local arts and
crafts and some items may even cause problems with customs officials back
home if they suspect the tortoiseshell is real.

Food and Drink

Not surprisingly, the main Maldivian source of protein is fish, mainly tuna and sailfish. Meals consist of a series of variations on the main staples: rice, fish and coconut. Because few islanders or even Malé residents have refrigerators, everything has to be prepared daily. On the islands, perishable food such as milk, butter, meat and fresh vegetables are not generally available unless specially arranged by the management. A local flat bread is prepared by grating coconut flesh and mixing it with flour before baking it on a thin sheet of tin over an open fire. Limes and chillis might be added to the fish to produce a curry that is normal breakfast fare. For the evening meal it's fish again, but this time as a thin soup to soak into the rice. Women on the islands spend much of their time husking imported rice and discarding seeds and stones.

Fish is prepared in many ways. *Hikumas* is fish which is first boiled and then smoked before being left in the sun for several hours; *valomas* is smoked fish; *fihunumas* is a barbecued preparation over which a paste of lime, coconut and chilli is applied before it is cooked over the fire. Dried fish is known as *telulimas*. The variations on this theme are many. *Kandu kukulu* is a fish curry. *Hana kuri* is prepared by frying the fish in spices until it is dry. *Garudiya* fish soup is the Maldivian national dish, made from a pungent treacle-like fish stock and served with rice, lime, onions, and green chilli. Concentrated fish stock is *rihakuru*. These dishes are commonly served with roti—plain flour pancakes like Indian chapatis. Maldivians serve fish for virtually every meal, including breakfast, which is usually *mas booli*, a dish made from grated coconut, fish, onion and chilli. The only green vegetable commonly grown on the islands is *murunga*. Curry leaves abound in the markets with *githeyo mirus*, a particularly virulent miniature capsicum that is a devilish *mirus* indeed!

Breadfruit is the commonest carbohydrate in the Maldivian diet, and is usually served fried; *bambukeylu hiti* is a special breadfruit curry. The starchy taro is also common, fried in slices as *ala*. Most exotic is the sweet fruit of the screw pine, which is mixed with bananas, sugar, and grated coconut. Highly popular is *diya hakuru,* a thick honey-like substance prepared from palu toddy, rice and bananas. This is especially popular during the days of Ramadan.

Maldivians like snacks, collectively called *hedhikaa*, though their sweet tooth is mercifully restrained. These are usually accompanied by a plate of betel leaves and lime paste. Favourites are *gulha*, fried fish balls made with an outer coating of rice or wheat flour; *kulhi boakiba*, a spicy fish cake with garlic and chilli; and *bajiya*, a samosa-shaped pastry stuffed with onion, fish, and coconut. A thick pancake made with flour, coconut, and sugar is known as a *folhi* and is often sweet; a *mas fatha fohli* is a smaller version of spicy fish cake and a *kulhi folhi* is a pancake mixed with a little *rihakuru* fish stock or turtle eggs. *Folhi boakiba* is a baked pastry with fried onions on top. *Foni roshi* is a sweet biscuit baked on a griddle like a chapati. Milk cakes are *kiru*, and *kiru sarbat* is a sweet milk drink traditionally taken with tea in tea shops.

The country is not especially rich in fruits though the screw pine's fruit is often sliced and eaten sweet, and three kinds of bananas can be found in the market in Malé, along with a sweet pistachio-like nut.

Unusual foods appear for special occasions. Special sweets and other dishes are enjoyed at Eid-ul-Fitr or Kuda Id the celebrations following Ramadan, the religious fasting month. These are also eaten following Malé circumcision ceremonies. Although western alcohol is heavily frowned upon, local brews can be quite inebriating.

The Maldivian toddy is called *raa* and is tapped from the crown of the palm trunk. It's a sweet and quite delicious drink if you can get over the pungent smell. Every village has its *raa vari* or toddy man, who shins up the trees to open their trunks with a machete.

Getting Around
From the Airport
Most visitors arrive in the Maldives on prearranged package tours that include the transfer from Hulule International Airport to the prepaid resort island. The type of transport provided depends on the distance, price of the tour, and type of resort. Expensive resorts like Cocoa Island and Nika provide a transfer by helicopter, hydrofoil, or high-speed launch. More modest resorts use *dhonis*, the traditional wooden all-purpose vessels of Maldivean waters—a lovely way to begin the transition towards total relaxation that most visitors crave.

Freer spirits can find their own way on private *dhonis* plying the ten-minute trip between Hulule airport and Malé for around Rf30 (about $3). There are regular ferries going from the airport to Malé almost hourly, except during meal times (12–3 pm and 5–7 pm). Arrangements can be made to hire a launch or speedboat for the same purpose at rates negotiable at the pierside.

In Malé
The capital is little more than a square mile in area, so the most practical way of getting around is to walk. Some cars, motorcycles and bicycles are available for hire. Taxis are also available but must be obtained by calling one of several taxi hire companies, or hailed from outside the Malé Government Hospital where they have a special stand. They do not cruise around town in search of fares. Taxi rates vary from Rf10-40 depending on the number of passengers and the amount of baggage.

By air

Air transport throughout the archipelago is intermittently provided by Air Maldives, whose two 18-seater Dornier 228s and single Sort Skyvan have scheduled flights five times per week to the distant islands of Gan, calling in twice-weekly at Kadhu and also at South Thiladhunmathi. Airports are under construction on Hadhdhumathi Atoll and North Miladhunmadulu Atoll. Better-off visitors may wish to make use of Hummingbird Helicopters, a private British company which operates transfers from the airport in a 24-seater helicopter. There are six helipads elsewhere in the Maldives. From these points tourists make the rest of the journey to their resort by speedboat or *dhoni*, which are included in their package price. This arrangement services some ten islands at present, but there are plans to expand the network and build new helipads in the near future. Rates are approximately $100 one-way, $200 return. Although it is usually arranged in advance with the resort, helicopter transport can be personally contracted. It is certainly the most spectacular way to arrive. The company also offers a 15-minute flight above the island and reefs of North Malé for $53. Contact them at: Luxwood, 2 Marine Drive, Malé (tel. 32-5708; fax. 32-3161).

By sea

Individual travellers who wish to charter a vessel to make their own way to resorts have a choice of traditional wooden *dhonis*, speed-boats, and motorized launches. All can be arranged either from representative offices or by haggling with individual boat owners at the pier in Malé. Prices tend to vary from high to very high, which is why this is not a popular option, running at around $150 for a day-long *dhoni* journey and the same for faster transportation.

The best established and most reliable company for hiring all of the above is ZSS. Many resorts can make arrangements to hire *dhonis*, speedboats, launches, and even yachts, for pleasure cruises, to explore surrounding islands, or for diving excursions. When island-bound inertia sets in this is the only way of breaking free in the Maldives. The costs vary with the type of vessel, the crew that accompanies it, and the amount of time you spend away (see Organizing a Boat Cruise, page 30).

It is a long time since the voyage from a remote island to Malé represented a major event in the lives of villagers who had to sail across the archipelago by *dhoni*, often for several weeks. Ferries and *vedis*, large wooden cargo boats, now ply between Malé and most inhabited islands throughout the 26 atolls in the Maldives. But they operate on an irregular basis and a non-Divehi speaking person will find it very hard to organize transport of this sort. Romantic illusions of being a hardy, adventurous traveller and 'going native' to explore the 'real' Maldives are likely to be shattered by reality. Although a ticket will cost next to nothing, it buys you several days of slow-boat life, chugging along through the surf on a hard bench with a brace of island families, a collection of livestock, and cargoes of smelly breadfruit and dried fish.

Although the past few years have seen some improvements in inter-island ferry and transport services, much remains to be done. Islanders are now demanding a faster mode of transport, and there is talk of hydrofoils and hover-craft soon replacing the old slow ferries. However, this may be wishful thinking and it is likely that transport to most parts of the Maldives will continue at its own slow pace for the foreseeable future.

Geography and Ecology

The Maldives is a chain of low coral atolls no more than 128 kilometres (80 miles) wide and stretching some 765 kilometres (475 miles) from north to south, running from latitude 7°N to just south of the equator. The country actually forms the central part of the Laccadive–Chagos Ridge, a submerged mountain range which is mostly about 300 metres (985 feet) deep. But the depth increases to more than 1,000 metres (3,280 feet) between the main part of the country and the two southernmost atolls.

The total land area is less than 300 square kilometres (115 square miles)—a tiny fraction of the 90,000 square kilometres within its official territory. The Laccadive, Minicoy, and Amindivi islands to the north—known collectively as Lakshadweep—belong to India, while the Chagos Archipelago to the south forms the British Indian Ocean Territory. The Maldives consists of about 1,200 islands together. Only nine are larger than two square kilometres (one square mile), and the biggest, Fuamulak, is just seven kilometres (four miles) at its widest point. Nowhere in the Maldives is more than four metres (15 feet) above mean sea level, so there are no hills or rivers and only one small freshwater lake.

Atoll Formation

The theory of atoll formation was first expounded by the great English naturalist, Charles Darwin, in 1842. Although he never visited the Maldives, Darwin made a close study of charts and other information about the area and described the differences between barrier and fringing reefs, and explained the creation of isolated atolls. In fact, the English word 'atoll' is derived from the Divehi word *atolu*.

Darwin's revolutionary view was that an atoll is not the coral-encrusted rim of a volcanic crater, as had been thought, but is formed when a small volcanic island, or tip of a mountain peak, gradually subsides into the sea. Coral grows in the warm, shallow water around this island, and as the sea level effectively rises, the coral growth keeps pace. Eventually, the original land disappears beneath the sea, leaving only the doughnut-shaped coral reef, or sting of islets, enclosing a central lagoon. The top part of the encircling reef is mostly exposed, and covered with accumulated coral sand and other debris. It has now become an island, or a series of islands, itself. There is a channel through the reef, linking the lagoon with the open sea, which is normally on the leeward side. (There is some argument about whether the land actually sinks, or whether the sea level rises, but this is relatively unimportant as both processes have probably been involved in atoll formation.)

In the last year of his life, Darwin expressed the hope that some 'doubly rich millionaire' would confirm his theory by making borings into a coral atoll. In due course, in 1952, the US Atomic Commission undertook just such a series of borings at Eniwetok Atoll, in the Pacific. The coral extended down for 1,220 metres (4,000 feet), and the underlying rock was found to contain fossilized shallow-water creatures, sure evidence that the rock had indeed changed position.

To this day, the atolls of the Maldives are considered the classical examples of coral atoll formation. And the Maldives has the largest true atoll in the world, the Huvadhu, which has a lagoon 112 kilometres (70 miles) in diameter, with a maximum depth of 86 metres (282 feet).

Malé's Problems

Conservation problems are usually concentrated where humans gather, and Malé is no exception. The key problem is its dwindling watertable of freshwater, a lens of relatively pure water beneath the soil surface that floats upon the denser saltwater held in the porous coral rock on which the city is built. This lens is deeper in the centre than the edges, so it looks like an upside down bowler hat. This has taken 15,000 years to establish, yet today the total rainfall throughout the entire Maldives archipelago would not be enough to satisfy ten weeks demand for water in Malé alone.

Since the recharge rate of Malé's aquifer is less than the rate of withdrawal it is now only possible to take freshwater from the centre of the island, supplemented by rooftop rain collection. The freshwater lens takes time to adjust to new levels, so an overpumped well can be fine for several years and then suddenly turn saline. Shallow wells draw the water-table level up even higher in a localised area, as a child's straw sucks up liquid in a glass, distorting the shape of the lens and rendering nearby wells useless. An improved drainage system can mean cleaner streets but it also stops the lens from recharging as easily as before. Salty storm water can be blown over the island, tainting the freshwater further. Malé's lens is now just 120 cm (four feet) below the surface and has a large and unusable brackish zone of contaminated water.

The signs are clear. The deep-rooted trees like breadfruit and mango suffer first. Sewage and pesticides are also a major factor affecting the purity of the source. On outer islands even the ubiquitous coconut is a headache. Coconuts transpire—lose to the atmosphere—a lot of water, around 70-130 litres (15–29 gallons) per tree every day; this compares with human consumption of 20-350 litres (four–76 gallons), a figure that rises to 1,000 (220 gallons) a day in some resorts. As *The Economist* noted in 1988, things are not helped by some Maldivians having two or three baths a day.

The mining of coral for construction purposes is also a worry; removal of the upper two metres (6.6 feet) of shallow reef flats on some islands in North Malé atoll is still carried out. It's estimated that at current rates of extraction, all the reefs in the North Malé atoll will be barren by the year 2014, with no recovery during the intervening period. It is no surprise that places like Edifushi in Baa

Organizing a Boat Cruise

The ultimate way to explore the Maldives is to hire your own luxury yacht-*dhoni*—a modern cross between a cargo boat and a cabin cruiser. This gives you total flexibility at all times, the chance to sleep where you choose, and the opportunity to experience the best aspects of a range of resorts as well as all the pleasures of relatively calm sea cruising. It is the favoured way to investigate the best diving spots of the Maldives, but there's no reason why you shouldn't just cruise around, if you can afford it.

The diving is best between the end of December and April. Charges are generally calculated per week, where everything bar the drinks—but including food—is paid inclusively if not in advance. The cost is about $50–80 per person per day. Most companies offer 'boat safaris' for a minimum of seven days, usually aiming for a ten-day cruise but often going out for up to three weeks. The most popular routes explore Ari Atoll. A two-week excursion goes as far as Felidhu. Each charter can handle four-12 people. The luxurious air-conditioned cabins are often beautifully fitted out with individual bathrooms, wardrobes, and finished in rattan-weave and dark mahogany wood. Or you can go downmarket for something more simple with a local look, and perfectly comfortable for a few days' cruising, with the local crew acting as chef, boat boys, and helmsmen.

The European-run charter companies provide on-board diving instructors in addition, and the three boats run by a trio of Italian skippers offer pasta freshly made in the galley. Contact can be made with the following:

Suntour Maldives. Giuseppe D'Amato operates a beautiful yacht, the *Baraa Baru,* which has four cabins suitable for ten people in all, with ensuite bathrooms, showers, television and video, and microwave cooking. This fully equipped diving dhoni can be hired out at around $100 per person per day.

Guido Villa can be contacted through Safari Tours or Agenzia Viaggi which run deals inclusive of air fare from Italy and transfers with Giorgio Rosi's company. Most travellers stay for one or two weeks, and most cruises concentrate on different diving locations.

Agenzia Detours operate four 20-metre (66-foot) and 24-metre (79-foot) yacht-*dhonis* with five or six cabins each. Every boat has its own smaller diving *dhoni*, air compressor, diving tanks, and enough diving equipment for up to 12 people. The Italian chef cooks fresh pasta, catches the fish, and specializes in lobster dishes. Hire charges start at about $120 per person per day, which includes two dives a day for safaris of 9-15 days (minimum of seven days). The company needs ten days' warning to get out of Kaafu to outlying atolls.

The major local operator in the Maldives is ZSS. They offer a diesel-powered dhoni for safari at $175 per day, dropping to $40 per person when shared by six or more. A slower boat starts at $130 per day. They also have two types of speedboat: a twin diesel capable of 35 knots at $440 per day with a capacity of ten people; and a smaller one with room for six at $350 for a full day. Yacht *dhonis* range from $250-350 depending on facilities, inclusive of taxes and meals (charged at $12 per person per day.) All boats are in radio contact with base. Diving equipment, including compressor, can be hired at around $75 per day.

Another alternative is a traditional dhoni run by a German called Asim, who married a Maldivian woman and became a Muslim. The boat—which he named *Shadas* after his wife—was used by the Norwegian explorer Thor Heyerdahl during his visits to the Maldives. It is now based at Rihiveli in South Malé Atoll and can be booked via tel. 32-4075 or tlx. 77025 REEFSIDE MF. It does not do diving trips but can advise on them.

Atoll have been selected as the first of the new islands to be colonized to escape Malé's dwindling water supplies and other headaches, and graced with a few extra feet of elevation to escape future inundation.

Coral

What we think of as coral is actually the external skeleton formed by a community of millions of tiny animals called 'polyps'. These coral polyps are diminutive members of a group of sea creatures, the coelenterates, which include jellyfishes, sea anemones, and sea fans. Snorkellers and divers usually cannot see the coral polyps, partly because they are generally extremely small, but also because they are mostly nocturnal and therefore retracted during the daytime. But if you have the necessary experience, do try a night dive, when you will see them expanded with their tentacles waving gently in the current. The tentacles are armed with stinging cells—nematocysts—which they shoot into passing prey to immobilize them. The prey animals, which are mostly microscopic planktionic creatures, but can also include tiny shrimps and even juvenile fishes, are then dragged by the tentacles into the mouth of the polyp.

But the life of the coral polyp has another important aspect, which helps explain its incredible reef-building powers. Inside the tissues of the polyp are symbiotic algae, that is, tiny plants literally 'living together' with the polyp to the mutual advantage of each. The algae use the sun's energy to convert carbon dioxide and water into oxygen and carbohydrates through the process called photosynthesis—and the coral polyp in turn makes good use of this supply of oxygen and extra food.

Besides the so-called 'hard corals', described above, there are also 'soft corals' which are somewhat similar but do not have the massive external skeleton. Instead, they produce a kind of internal skeleton formed in limestone crystals. And some of the soft corals do not have the symbiotic algae of the hard, reef-building corals. One further point is that since algae depend on sunlight, and sunlight is quickly absorbed by seawater, it is rare to find much hard coral growing deeper than 30 metres (100 feet). After that, soft corals, sponges and other organisms that do not depend on the sun's rays start to take over.

The limestone skeleton of the hard coral remains even when the polyps die, and it is this which forms the permanent structure we know as a coral reef. The reefs of the Maldives—and, indeed, they are the life the country—have been constructed over millenia by huge armies of tirelessly energetic coral polyps. Ooover 200 different species of hard coral are found in the Maldives—which contributes to the diversity of the reef, and of course creates an endless variety of habitats for an astonishing range of colourful underwater creatures.

The coral reef as a whole is an immensely complex ecosystem, and the interactions and survival strategies of its inhabitants are endlessly varied—and

deeply fascinating, for those underwater explorers with the inclination to observe and try to understand their behaviour. Most relationships that are likely to be seen are based on predator-prey interactions. However, there are some other relationships likely to be seen by the diver which are more harmonious. These include the association between clown fishes and potentially lethal anemones, and the mutually beneficial system known as 'cleaning symbiosis'.

Clown fish are brightly coloured fish, usually yellowish with a distinctive blue stripe, that are found hovering above or often half hidden amongst the venomous tentacles of sea anemones. The fish protects itself from harm by secreting a mucus that disguises its own chemical composition, and at the same time covering itself with the anemone's own mucus. Thus, the anemone is deceived into thinking that the fish is actually part of itself. The benefit to the clown fish of this arrangement is that it is protected by the anemone's tentacles. While the benefit to the anemone is not quite so obvious, it is probable that the anemone is not bothered by potential predators because the presence of the brightly coloured clown fish warns them away.

Swimming around the reef, one can soon spot established 'cleaner stations' where small fishes are diligently at work cleaning parasites, dead tissues, and fungus off larger species. The cleaners work over their customers' bodies, including the gill cavities and even inside the mouth, without risk of harm. In fact, the client species often seem to enjoy the experience, and are protective towards the cleaners (who also benefit by getting a meal in the process). Sometimes quite large numbers of bigger fishes will gather at the cleaning stations and it is amusing to see them wait their turn in an orderly fashion.

Besides full-time cleaners (usually species of cleaner wrasse in the Maldives), there are some which only perform this function on a part-time basis and others, such as angelfish and butterflyfish, that do it only while they are juveniles. The cleaners also include invertebrates, especially shrimps.

Fishes Large and Small

Apart from the beauty of the reefs themselves—and many people consider the reefs of the Maldives to be the most beautiful in the world—probably their greatest attraction is the dazzling variety and number of fishes that inhabit them.

First the lagoon, which in a typical atoll is surrounded by the reef. A surprising variety of fishes can be found here, often at depths of no more than 1.5 metres (five feet). Though the bottom is mainly sandy—not normally a good place to find fishes—there are outcroppings of coral that act as magnets for fish. Here you will see damselfishes and clown fish, including the blackfooted clown fish which is unique to the area, and juveniles of many other colourful reef species, especially surgeonfish, triggerfish, and wrass. You may also encounter young whitetip reef sharks in this nursery area. If you have never met a shark before, and are uneasy at the prospect, this is a good place to start, as the youngsters may only measure a metre (three feet) or so, and should allow you to conquer your fears in readiness for the big-time world of the reef itself.

Once outside the lagoon on the seaward side of the protective reef, everything changes. At first you will be awed by the sheer number and diversity of fish. More than 1,000 species have been recorded from the Maldives and the surrounding ocean, so it is one of the most species-rich marine areas of the world. With this abundance, you may find your first experience of fish watching bewildering. What you can be sure of is that each dive will be different, bringing new and colourful and sometimes surprising sights. You will want to keep returning again and again, so much is there to see.

There are fishes of all sizes in the Maldives, from very small ones like the brilliant-coloured fire goby to the massive manta ray and the gigantic humphead wrasse which is the length of a tall man but much heavier, up to 190 kilograms (420 pounds). If you are lucky, you might encounter the largest fish of all, the harmless, plankton-feeding whale shark, which can attain a length of about 12 metres (40 feet) and weigh more than 20 tonnes.

But more likely you will meet those colourful and characteristic reef fishes, the angelfishes and their close relatives the butterflyfish; the former are mostly seen on their own, while schools of pennant butterfly fish numbering several hundred are not uncommon. There are plenty of large gropers, of which a striking example is the vermilion rock cod, bright red or orange and decorated with a maze of blue spots. Schools of surgeonfish graze the coral walls of the reef (look for the beautiful powder blue surgeonfish) while large-eyed, nocturnal soldierfish and their cousins the squirrelfish, hang out under ledges. And you can be sure to see jack, snapper, goatfish, fusilier, anthias, coral-crunching parrotfish (you can actually hear them doing it), and a host of others.

There are some special sights to look forward to in the Maldives. Unicornfish are fairly common here, though not so elsewhere. The aptly named cowfish, a member of the boxfish family, has pairs of 'horns' pointing fore and aft. The large red-faced batfish is a companionable creature, and it is not unusual for a group of them to escort divers while they explore the reef.

Sharks, turtles, green, loggerhead, leatherback, and especially hawksbill turtles are relatively common and an underwater encounter with one of these great amphibians is an outstanding experience. Ungainly on land—and it is only the females who ever return to the beach to lay their eggs—some turtles can reach speeds of 50 kph (31 mph) or more in the sea.

Among other denizens of Maldivian reefs there are slow-moving lionfish, beautiful but poisonous—though easy to avoid—and sharp-toothed moray eels poking out of holes in the coral. Although quite harmless unless you harrass them, it is probably wise not to temp fate by touching a moray eel, as some people do, for it has a grip of steel and you would never be able to pull free if it did choose to bite your arm. Starfish, brittle starts, feather starts, sea urchins, sea cucumbers, sea squirts and hermit crabs are just some of the other life forms to be seen and enjoyed.

Land Animals and Birds

Compared with the astonishing richness of the marine life, the terrestrial fauna of the Maldives is very limited, in common with other oceanic islands. Nevertheless, it is quite interesting, though as yet little studied.

Most of the animals have come to the Maldives from India or Sri Lanka, and indeed all of the mammals and reptiles are also found in those two countries except the fruit bat, or flying fox, which is judged to be a distinct Maldivian sub-species. The fruit bat no doubt made its own way to the Maldives, but the other mammals—the black rat, house mouse, and Indian house shrew—were almost certainly introduced by man or came on ships. There are also a few cats and goats, but no dogs as these are not allowed on religious and health grounds.

The reptiles, which may also have been introduced, include two nocturnal house geckos, a colourful agamid lizard that is fairly common on some islands, a skunk, and two nonpoisonous snakes. In addition, there is one species of frog and one toad. Little is known about the invertebrates, but there are nearly 70 species of butterflies.

Birds are more numerous, with more than a hundred different kinds recorded, but only a small proportion of these breed in the islands. The two commonest land birds are the house crow and the koel, a cuckoo that depends on the crow as host for its eggs. These are present on most of the inhabited islands, including Malé, and the resort islands. The crow has increased to pest proportions but no effective method of control has yet been found. The crow is easily seen, and its harsh *caw* is just as easily heard. The koel by contrast is seldom seen, though its varied and remarkable repertoire of calls (some sound like a girl screaming) are unmistakable.

There is a total absence of small passerine birds. However, the nonindigenous rose-ringed parakeet, bright green with a red bill is a colourful sight on Malé and nearby islands. The only other land bird likely to be seen is the rather elusive white-breasted waterhen, which nests under low bushes and rank vegetation in the centre of some islands in Mahe Atoll.

Some 13 different herons are found in the Maldives, the commonest being the large grey heron, which stands on the outer reefs of most islands waiting patiently for a suitable meal to swim by. Some of the other herons are thought to be endemic subspecies.

Most numerous are the seabirds, among which are several terns including the graceful fairy tern (though this is confined to Addu Atoll in the south). Two frigate birds breed in the Maldives in small numbers, the great and the lesser; two noddies (which fishermen watch out for as they indicate where the tuna are); Audubon's shearwater; and one of the most elegant of seabirds, the white-tailed tropic bird. It is possible the red-tailed and red-billed tropic birds also breed here.

A number of migrant birds, and others that have been blown off course, visit the Maldives at various time of the year. They include petrels, shearwaters, ducks, various birds of prey, and such birds as whimbrels, plovers and sand pipers.

Plants

As with the animal life, the Maldives are not rich in terrestrial plant species. Of about 600 species, more than half were probably introduced for food or other human use, such as herbs, in medicine or as ornamental plants or shade trees. Others are common tropical plants that are often found in association with man. It has been estimated that less than 100 species might have colonized the islands before the arrival of man.

Even including all the introductions, the Maldives has far fewer plant species than it has islands, unlike the situation in most tropical island groups. The explantion may be that in the low-lying Maldives there are not many different ecological niches available, and thus only limited possibilities for plant colonization. One very interesting point, which has been noted by Dr Dennis Adams of the Natural History Museum in London, is that most of the common native plants of the Maldives are also found on similar islands in the Pacific—but are rare or absent in between. He suggests that they reached the Maldives from the Pacific, rather than the other way round.

Only five of the Maldivian plants are said to be true endemic species (not found anywhere else), and these are the local varieties of pandanus, or screw pine. The question is still open, however, as it seems unlikely that these trees alone should be endemic, especially as their seeds are very well adapted for oceanic dispersal. Furthermore the Maldivians themselves do not recognize five kinds of pananus but three, which they identify as small, medium and large.

Of cultivated plants, the visitor may see breadfruit, mango, tamarind, areca nut palms, lime, watermelon, pineapple and banana. Crops include millet, some sorghum, sweet potato, taro, manioc, and Indian arrowroot. Rice is not grown, but substantial quantities are imported.

History

Local historians place the first major settlement in the Maldives around the fifth century BC, part of the great Aryan drive southwards and eastwards from the Indus valley in northwestern India. They encountered some people of Dravidian stock already living on the islands, Hindus marooned on the archipelago by shipwreck and circumstance. The Aryans introduced their language *ellu*, a pure form of the Sinhalese spoken in present-day Sri Lanka, and their religion, Buddhism. It is thought that the name 'Maldives' derives from a Sanskrit word *malodheep* meaning garland. Buddhist relics, statuary, carvings, and mounds have been found on at least 60 large islands in the archipelago though no list has been compiled. The eight largest such relics are Nilandhu in Faafu Atoll, Isdu and Fuamulaku in Laamu, Gan in Gaaf Dhall, Kibidhu in Thaa, Thoddu in Alifu, and Landu in Noonu. Landu has one compound with seven stupas of different sizes, including a big one on a raised platform. Archaeological efforts are hampered by a lack of experts to supervise digs. Some Portuguese relics have also been found on Hitadu in Seenu Atoll, Guraidu in Thaa, Kolhufushi in Meemu, Utimu in Haaa-Alifu, and Fuamulaku in Gnaviyani.

Heyerdahl's Theories

The famous Norwegian anthropologist-explorer, Thor Heyerdahl, had a particular fascination with the Maldives. His curiosity was aroused by pictures sent to him of a statue featuring a man's head with the hair braided in a top knot and ears extending down to his shoulders. The figure was obviously Buddhist in origin, but bore a striking resemblance to figures Heyerdahl had investigated on Easter Island in the Pacific Ocean. Obviously they were not part of Maldivian post-Islamic culture as no representation of the body is allowed in Muslim worship. Where did they come from?

Heyerdahl's conclusion is that the Maldives lay at the crossroads of the great east-west trade routes linking pre-Christian Europe and the Near Eastern civilizations with China and the East Indies. Anyone travelling from east to west would have had to pass through the archipelago. Evidence of this movement, as much as 4,000 years ago, turns up in unlikely places and shows that whoever colonized the Maldives were a civilized people, not simply untutored, ship-wrecked sailors. The **hawitta** mound (like a Buddhist stupa) on Nilandu dates back to about AD 500. Two thousand years earlier, peoples in northwest India and the Indus valley had begun a series of migrations, including south to Sri Lanka and beyond. They were experts in carving solid rock into precision-fitting blocks without masonry, they sculpted lions and bulls, and used the swastika and lotus for decorations, all of which have been found in the Maldives. The phallic stones also unearthed in the Maldives date back to the Indus civilization, the shape prefiguring the representation of Shiva, the important Hindu deity.

The Power of Faith

*T*rustworthy men among the inhabitants, such as the lawyer Isa al-Yamani, *the lawyer and school-master* Ali, *the* Kází Abd Allah, *and others, related to me that the people of these islands used to be idolaters, and that there appeared to them every month an evil spirit, one of the Jinn, who came from the direction of the sea. He resembled a ship full of lamps.* The custom of the natives, as soon as they *perceived him, was to take a young virgin, to adorn her, and to conduct her to the* budkhána, *that is to say, an idol temple, which was built on the sea-shore and had a window by which she was visible. They left her there during the night and returned in the morning, at which time they were wont to find the young girl dishonoured and dead. Every month they drew lots, and he upon whom the lot fell gave up his daughter. At length arrived among them a Maghrabin Berber, called* Abú'l-barakát, *who knew by heart the glorious Koran. He was lodged in the house of an old woman of the island* Mahal [Male]. *One day he visited his hostess and found that she had assembled her relatives, and that the women were weeping as at a funeral. He questioned them upon the subject of their affliction, but they could not make him understand the cause, until an interpreter, who chanced to come in, informed him that the lot had fallen upon the old woman, and that she had an only daughter, who was now about to be slain by the evil Jinni.* Abú'l-barakát *said to the woman: 'I will go to-night in thy daughter's stead.' At that time he was entirely beardless. So, on the night following, after he had completed his ablutions, he was conducted to the idol temple. On* *arrival there he set himself to recite the Koran. Presently, through the window, beholding the demon to approach, he continued his recitation. The Jinni, as soon as he came within hearing of the Koran, plunged into the sea and disappeared; and so it was that, when the dawn was come, the Maghrabin was still occupied in reciting the Koran. When the old woman, her relatives, and the people of the island, according to their custom, came to take away the girl and burn the corpse, they found the stranger reciting the Koran. They conducted him to their King, by name Shanúrdza, whom they informed of this adventure. The King was astonished; and the Maghrabin both proposed to him to embrace the true faith, and inspired him with a desire for it. Then said Shanúrdza to him: 'Remain with us until next month, and if you do again as you have now done and escape the evil Jinni, I will be converted'. Wherefore the stranger remained with the idolaters, and God disposed the heart of the King to receive the true faith. He became Musalmán before the end of the month, as well as his wives, children, and courtiers. At the beginning of the following month the Maghrabin was conducted again to the idol temple; but the Jinni came not, and the Berber recited the Koran till the morning, when the Sultan and his subjects arrived and found him so employed. Then they broke the idols, and razed the temple to the ground. The people of the island embraced Islam, and sent messengers to the other islands, whose inhabitants were also converted.*

Ibn Battuta, translated by Albert Gray, 1888

As for the cowrie shells found in Scandinavia as far north as the Arctic Circle in graves dating back 1,500 years, these seem to have been passed on by Arab traders to nomadic peoples from Finland in exchange for furs. Chinese pottery shards found on the beaches in some southern Maldive islands date from the Sung and Ming dynasties, and are therefore between 450 and 1,000 years old. One fragment, though, has been identified as Neolithic and of a type that ceased to exist about 2,000 BC. Roman coins dating from the time of Christ have also been recorded, and written records from the fourth century mention people calling themselves 'the *divi*' paying homage to a new emperor. The first-century historian Pliny recorded also how the Egyptians made their way to India in order to trade, and used the changeable monsoon winds to bring them back in under a year of travel. The old Maldivian system of counting, using a base of 12 instead of ten, may have been taken from Mesopotamia, site of the old civilizations of Babylon and Sumer.

Records in Sri Lanka talk of a migration west to some coral atolls around 500 BC, at the instigation of a Buddhist seer, so the Sinhalese probably shared the settlement of the Maldives with Hindus from the far north of India 2,500 years ago. The last, and still unsolved mystery, concerns the identity of a group of mound and temple-builders known in Maldivian oral legend as 'the Redin', a white-skinned, brown-haired people with big bones and blue eyes, tall people with long faces who worshipped the statues they made and who came east down the pathway of the sun, sounding uncannily like the pre-Columbians of Mexico and Peru. One such **hawitta** on Gaaf-Gan appears to be solar-oriented, a square with steps, three lion heads and a relief of a bull.

Perhaps this mystery will never be solved. Unfortunately, almost all the carvings and mounds have been destroyed, either to make new buildings or through religious fanaticism.

Myth of the Conversion

The Maldives were almost certainly converted to Islam over a period of time. Perhaps as much as a century passed before the belief had spread throughout the archipelago and fully displaced Buddhism. Nonetheless, Maldivians have a strong deliverance myth of this event, which also served to reinforce the righteous power of the new religion over the old superstitions. The Arabic traveller, Ibn Battuta, recorded a legend about two centuries after the twelfth-century conversion that demonstrates the virtue of true Islamic belief.

The legend states that the capital was suffering from the predations of a *rannamari*, a demon of the sea who began plaguing Malé in 1153, threatening to destroy the town unless a virgin was sacrificed every month. The king at the time, one Kalaminja, was forced to accede to these requests until an itinerant Moroccan trader called Abul Baaketh Yusuf el-Barbary worked out a way to save them. Disturbed that one of the daughters of the house where he was lodging was next on the rota for sacrifice, Abul decided to take her place. Making his way at night to the temple assigned for the deed, and disguised as a girl, he passed most of the hours of darkness by an open window piously reciting verses from the Koran. When at last he saw the spirit rising from the waters he merely began reciting the verses even louder, causing the demon to squeal with pain and disappear below the waters forever. Not surprisingly, Abul soon persuaded King Kaliminja to convert to the religion that had so amply demonstrated its powers, which the king did, taking the title Sultan Muhammad Ibn Abdullah. He is said to have ruled for 25 years and founded a dynasty, only to disappear suddenly on a pilgrimage to Mecca.

A second version, related in the ancient Maldivian chronicle, the *Tarikh*, tells how Sheik Yusuf Shamsuddin of Tabriz, a renowned and pious man, came to the Maldives and conjured up a jinni as big as the sky on the 12th day of Rabi-ul-Akhir, Anno Hajjirae 548, that is AD 1153, which persuaded everyone from the king down to become Muhammadans.

Islamic Kingdom

Despite the Maldives strategic location it has not been the prey of successive foreign powers, possibly because the shallowness of the lagoons and the difficulty of navigation without intimate knowledge of the waters protected the country from interference. Modern historians like to date the Maldives as a defined political identity from the era of the conversion, which would make it the oldest small state in the world outside a brace of anachronisms in Europe.

Life was blissfully event free until 1495 when a deposed ruler, Sultan Kulu Mohamed ('the black'), turned to the king of the Malabars for assistance in regaining his throne. It is unclear whether this was given the first time this sultan was deposed, for he certainly regained his title at one point only to lose it again. But on this occasion Malabari troops certainly were used, together with Portuguese soldiers they met on the short voyage from southern India to the Maldives. This alliance proved costly to the Sultan, as the Portuguese claimed an annual tribute payable to their viceroy in Goa, which later led them to establish a presence in Malé by force in 1517, in effect annexing the country. This first European foray was cut short by troops lent by the ruler of Cochin.

Freedom was short lived, however, as a few years later another ruler, Sultan Hassan IX, was deposed after showing too little respect for Islam. Fleeing to Cochin, he was met by the Jesuit missionary, St Francis Xavier who baptized him a Christian and renamed him Don Emanuel. He stayed in Cochin for two years before moving up the coast to Goa where he married a Portuguese noblewoman. Aided by the troublesome Portuguese, former Sultan Hassan-Emanuel led two expeditions to regain control over the Maldives: both were unsuccessful.

In fact, the Portuguese had ideas of their own for the Maldives and in 1558 sent an expedition under a Captain Andreas Andre. According to Maldivian

legend, this commander was born in the Maldives, his mother being the wife of a ship's captain who was also commander of the forces raised against Kulu Umbushumu who in turn destroyed the Portuguese fleet and killed everyone on board except this woman, Captain Andre's mother. Taking her to his island, he later married her; her child grew up to be known as Andiri Andirin.

As a young man he escaped to Goa, only to return years later as commander of the Portuguese forces. He annihilated the Maldivians under Sultan Ali VI, who died in the heat of battle, while fortifying himself from a coconut full of toddy.

The Portuguese

For the next 17 years, the Portuguese under Andreas Andre were the rulers of the Maldives, in the name of King Hassan-Emanuel. Local historians brood over this period as the darkest hour of their nation's history, a time when men were treated as slaves, women were violated at whim, deputies extended a reign of terror to the outer atolls, and the Europeans generally tried to force everyone to become Christian. François Pyrard de Laval notes thoughtfully, however, that people told him only a few decades later that trade had never been as good as when the Portuguese were in charge.

Redemption for the Maldives came in the form of Mohamed Thakurufaanu, born on the distant island of Utheemu, and prophetically on the very same day as Andreas Andre. He and his two brothers, one of whom was beheaded by the Portuguese, built a fast boat in which they embarked upon a form of guerilla warfare—hit-and-run tactics that weakened the Portuguese without challenging them seriously (though one local historian has suggested their feats were 'sometimes bordering on the supernatural').

Malé, they decided, was too hard for them to take on single-handed so they sought assistance from the Rajah of Cannanore. Thakurufaanu returned in 1573 on the night a Portuguese ultimatum to the Maldivian elders expired. This obliged them to convert to Christianity or be put to the sword. Placing his Malabari troops in positions around the town, he managed to infiltrate a party into the Portuguese encampment and shoot Andre from behind a coconut tree—a nice Maldivian touch that makes the legend seem quite real, especially as miraculously the tree also deflected the bullet that Andre fired back. A fierce battle ensued in which the Portuguese were all killed, eventually leaving Thakurufaanu in charge as Sultan Ghazi Muhammad Thakurufan al-Auzam.

The Portuguese tried on several further occasions to retake the Maldives in order to install a puppet regime with the grandchildren of King Hassan-Emanuel. These all failed, after which the Portuguese left the Maldives in peace. Thakurufaanu ruled with his brother, eventually dying in 1585. He is credited with having minted the first local coins, forming a trained standing army, and improving religious observance and trade.

Thakurufaanu's son, Sultan Kalaafannu, fared less fortunately and was killed by a bunch of marauding Malibari pirates who caught him on the high seas fleeing south and then proceeded to plunder Malé and destroy the royal palace. An official expedition was mounted in the mid-seventeenth century by the Rajah of Cannanore when Sultan Iskander I withheld payment of the tribute that had been paid for over a century and a half since the time of Sultan Kulu Muhammad. After a brief struggle the position was reversed, with the Maldivian sultan persuading the inhabitants of Minicoy, a small group of islands just north of the Maldives and under the Rajah's rule, to pay him tribute instead.

Pyrard's Adventures

François Pyrard de Laval was a Frenchman who sailed in 1601 from St Malo en route for the East Indies. Fourteen months after leaving France his ship, the *Corbin*, was shipwrecked on a Maldivian reef while the captain was sick and the watch drunk or asleep. Some of the crew escaped only to be flung into the Portuguese galleys, but Pyrard himself was held captive in Malé for five years, earning the trust of the sultan by his alacrity in learning the language. Eventually he was rescued by a fleet from Chittagong which arrived to try to salvage the *Corbin's* cannons.

Pyrard then began his long journey home which serendipitously took him to Brazil before finally landing in Spain in 1611, a decade after he left Europe. His account, the first full-length one of the Maldives and the Malabar coast of India, made him famous. It has only been matched by an account by two British naval officers, Christopher and Powell, who visited the islands in the 1830s.

The story he unfolds is of an autocratic sultan to whom everything ship-wrecked on the many reefs belonged, and for whose subjects it was treason to leave the country without permission. However, Pyrard became something of a celebrity at court, the sultan's wives asking him many questions about the French court and being amazed that the French king only had one wife. He found the people 'cunning in trade and in social life'. The women grew their hair long, well oiled, and stuffed with false hair culled from the menfolk of the Malibars. Hirsute men were despised; children of both sexes had theirs shorn every week until the age of nine, and old men shaved their torsos into strange patterns as though they were wearing a slashed doublet. Pyrard's main complaint was that they used blunt razors that always drew blood, though everyone pretended—with Maldivian machismo—that it didn't hurt at all.

He learned Divehi, and some Arabic which he observed is learned 'by them as Latin is with us.' He recorded the love rituals of gifts of betel and sonnets between youngsters, and the rule that a man with three wives must sleep with all three equally regularly. 'It is but an ill-considered law for these countries where three husbands would not suffice for one wife, so lewd are the women,' he observed caustically. An anthropologist with an eye for fashion, Pyrard noted the silk petticoats and the robes of taffeta or fine cotton, and the gold bracelets that could only be worn with the permission of the sultana. He noted also the women's winsome figures, that they were always well turned out, and the 'country notion of beauty' of painting their toe and fingernails red.

Pyrard was impressed by the Maldivians' consistent hospitality among themselves and their fastidiousness in preparing food and eating, and their habit of discarding broken crockery which they used instead of gold and silver (as this was forbidden, even for the sultan). He was similarly horrified by their rampant superstition and by 'their indulgence of women, lascivious and intemperate'. He wrote that 'adultery, incest and sodomy are common, notwithstanding the severity of the law and penalties. . . the women are strangely wanton, and the men no better. . . their chief desire is to find, if they can, some recipe where-withal to satisfy their wives. . . and I believe they would give all their substance for such a thing. They have often asked me if I knew of any such means, even the highest nobles, and so often, that I was quite sick of the subject'. He added that they were addicted to opium and that common talk of sex was shunned. Politely, he forbears to describe this as straightforward hypocrisy.

He observed summary judgments in the courts and lashings, along with the orchards and gardens of the king's palace, the raised floors to escape the ants and the beds suspended from the ceiling so as to rock the wealthy to sleep. Apparently the sultana and her retinue lived behind five hangings of cloth in an apartment without natural light.

All was peaceful in the Maldives until 1752 when the younger brother of Iskander I, Sultan Muhammad Imaduddin III, was deposed by invading Malibaris under Ali Rajah for about four months. Then another hero, Hassan Manikfan, duped the Malibaris into retiring to bed early one night and massa-cred the lot of them. When the rajah sent another force to retake Malé, Hassan ran up the Malibari flag at the port entrance and sent out a welcoming party disguised as Malibaris, conning the fleet into entering the harbour unawares only to be destroyed by cannon fire. A third invasion was foiled after Hassan enlisted the help of the French at Pondicherry under Captain Le Termellier and the Dutch who helped destroy the Malibari fleet at sea. Hassan in time became Sultan Al Ghazi Hassan Izzaddin.

The British

Relative freedom lasted until 1887 when Sultan Muhammad Muenuddin signed an agreement with the British governor of Ceylon turning the Maldives into a British protectorate on payment of an annual tribute. This arrangement left the sultans ruling as autocrats until 1932 when a new constitution was adopted and a republic briefly declared. However, royal power returned soon afterwards. Following the independence of India and Sri Lanka after the Second World War, the British dropped the requirement for tribute, and finally a republic was declared in 1953. The first president, Amin Didi, was, however, overthrown after a coup and died a prisoner on Vihamanafushi, now the resort island of Kurumba. Once again the Maldives reverted to a sultanate.

The British, however, were interested in using the strategic southern atolls and established an RAF base on Gan in 1957, an unpopular decision in Malé which led to the resignation of the prime minister. This coincided with a period of unrest in the three southernmost atolls which felt the central authorities in far-off Malé were making life unduly harsh for them, especially by forcing them to call in at Malé before sailing off to trade with India and Sri Lanka. A rebel government in the south declared itself independent as the United Suvadive Atolls under one Abdulla Afeef; it managed to hold out against government forces without guns for around four years, but in the end was spirited away to exile in the Seychelles.

The British continued leasing the airfield facilities on Gan until 1976, when the Labour government decided it was too expensive to maintain. The Russians then said they wanted to use Gan—450 miles north of the strategic US naval and air base on Diego Garcia—for the Soviet fishing fleet. They offered the Maldivians a small rent, but President Nasir upped the price and asked for $1 million. According to a report in the *Asian Wall Street Journal*, a Soviet diplomat complained angrily to a Western colleague that 'you could buy the whole country for $1 million'. And so the deal fell through. Maldivians remember things differently, viewing the rent as bait to allow the Russians to avoid Maldivian customs and immigration checks, which would have effectively barred Maldivians from Gan altogether.

Independence

The Maldives were granted full independence on 26 July 1965. The reigning sultan, the 94th, Muhammad Fareed I, lasted another three years before a republic was declared after a referendum, and the hero of the anti-British protests, Ibrahim Nasir, became the first president. He held office until his resignation in 1978, followed by his sudden departure and self-imposed retirement in Singapore. He was later sentenced to 25 years' banishment in absentia for fermenting rebellion and plotting a coup.

President Maumoon Abdul Gayoom, the current incumbent, has been re-elected twice, the last occasion being in 1988 with more than 96 percent of the vote, an achievement unmatched outside of the former Soviet satellite countries of eastern Europe. He was the target of a second coup attempt in November 1988, when a tropical fish exporter, Abdulla Luthufi, tried to seize power using mercenaries from one of the Tamil independence factions in neighbouring Sri Lanka. The mercenaries proved very incompetent, and the insurrection was finally put down by Rajiv Gandhi's troops during one of the Indian leader's expansionary phases. Dozens of people were sentenced to death

and later banished after public trials in Malé a year later.

Gayoom manages to mention the coup attempt every time foreign dignitaries come to Malé, even proclaiming the coup attempt day a new public holiday. Meanwhile a dissident group calling itself the White Sharks has re-emerged after a ten-year silence, accusing Gayoom's government of nepotism and corruption, and clandestinely distributing leaflets outside the mosques that detail the bank balances of senior government ministers.

Since achieving independence in 1965, the Maldives has charted an independent course for itself as a member of the British Commonwealth, a non-aligned state within the United Nations, and a loyal Muslim nation. It ranks as the 117th state in the United Nations and is its smallest member.

Changing Times

Malé enjoyed something of a boom in the 1970s when hundreds of Indian traders made regular visits to take advantage of the duty-free regulations, a form of commuter smuggling that the Indians cracked down on after a few years. The dried fish industry boomed for a while but collapsed just as the tourist industry was getting off the ground in 1972. Government policy now is to push the resorts up-market, to get the 'value-added' tourist. Backpackers are strictly discouraged. Under President Nasir, islands could be sold outright, but this policy was changed in the 1980s and the 'lost' islands nationalized. Resorts are now leased by the government, instead of being sold.

Much recent construction work, such as the airport runway extension, has been funded by loans from friendly Arab nations like Saudi Arabia. Malé's breakwater was rebuilt in 1987 partly with Japanese money, and partly with a loan from the Asian Development Bank, which is basically Japanese-funded.

Many people feel the Maldives is changing rapidly. The days when massive sail-driven *buggalows* took three days to sail to Sri Lanka are now a distant memory. Traditions of warmth and hospitality—especially the practice of *mutaa*, or short-term marriage of convenience—have often been abused by visitors in the past. So nowadays, for example, a foreigner who wishes to marry a Maldivian has to change his religion and name, become a Muslim, and register these facts on his passport.

Life in the Maldives has certainly changed, but compared with the recent past much of the change has been distinctly positive. In 1965 there were no social welfare programmes in the Maldives. There was a high rate of infant mortality and communicable diseases were prevalent. Yet by 1977, life expectancy had been raised from 46 to 62 years, and infant mortality cut by a third. While English had been banned by the sultans until as recently as 50 years ago, an English language school was established in Malé in 1961.

Culture

Maldivian myths and folklore are focused on the sea, reflecting the local lifestyle which revolves around the changing seasons and the size of the fishing catch—as befits a tiny, remote island nation. This natural rhythm is threatened, however, as with other isolated cultures, by the increase of international tourism, the importation of western goods, and the evidence of growing wealth accumulated by some islanders. Many young Maldivians dream of making it big in Malé rather than staying in a small fishing village in a far-flung atoll. Looked at another way, today's international tourists are just the latest in a long history of visitors which started with the earliest traders two millenia or more ago. These early traders, whose boats made use of favourable winds to round the tip of the Indian subcontinent to ply between the East Indies and Africa, are long gone, but their influence and presence can still be felt.

Maldivians, or the *Divi* as they were known to ancient Roman and Arabic chroniclers, are a Dravidian people, a mix of Indian, Sinhalese, and Tamil cultures with even earlier roots reaching back to East Africa and Arabia. Modern historians believe the strongest affinities are with the Sinhalese of Sri Lanka, whose ancestors spoke an Indo-Aryan language and originally sailed south from the northwest Indian coast. The earliest inhabitants of Sri Lanka, however, were Tamil speakers, and according to the explorer Thor Heyerdahl, many words in the Maldivian language, especially those to express kinship and the finer points of ocean navigation, are obviously Tamil in origin. The word *dhoni* for example, comes from Tamil.

It is believed that the very first settlers of the Maldives—mostly lost fishermen, shipwrecked sailors, and their descendants from South India—were Hindu. But the Aryans who colonized the islands later brought their own religion and a language called *ellu*, a Sanskrit-based language which is close to a very pure form of the Sinhalese spoken in Sri Lanka today.

Divehi Script and Language

The Maldives' official language is called *Divehi*, which also gives its name to the country, *Divehi raajje* '(Divehi speakers), and the people *Divehin* '(islanders). Although this is derived from the *ellu* tongue, it can be considered a corruption of Sanskrit, the language that spread out from the Indus Valley region after the year 1,500 BC as the great Indo-Aryan civilization collapsed, extending across most of the subcontinent and the Near East. Present-day *Divehi* has acquired words from other sources, including Malayalam, Arabic, and Tamil.

The earliest Maldivian script was known as *evayla* and was written left to right in the same manner as the roman script. This was superceded by another called *dives akuru*, which was also written from left to right, and which was itself replaced four centuries ago by the script in current use, called *thaana akuru*, which has more Arabic-style characters and has changed to right to left to accommodate them.

Although Arabic letters had been familiar since the introduction of the Koran 800 years ago, the Maldivians have continued using their own *thaana* script. They were obviously a literate nation even before the Arabs came and examples of their earliest script are preserved in several ancient copper books known as *loamaafaanu*, the earliest of which dates back to 1195. The modern *thaana* script resembles a series of tiger paw prints, or a snake wriggling across the sand, fat squiggles which do not appear as refined or elegant as the scimitar-thin swirls and loops of classical Arabic. Like other language forms, including Chinese, there's no exact correlation between *thaana* and our roman script so modern spellings of the same word or name can vary enormously; thus *Dhivehi* and *Divehi* are both in common usage.

A borrower from many tongues, as befits its trading crossroads history, *Divehi* has only donated one word—atoll—that has made its way into everyday use in the English language. This name for an island fringed by a reef and enclosing a shallow lagoon was passed into English by returning sailors, and is a good example of the need for a loan word as such conditions are not found in the seas around the British Isles.

Creatures of the Deep

hey have an admirable quantitie of great Fish, as Bonitos, Albachores, guilt-heads and others which are very like one another, and of the same taste, and have no more skales then the Mackrell. They take them in the deepe Sea, on this fashion, with a line of a fathom and a halfe of great round Cotton thred made fast to a great Cane. Their hooke, is not so much bowed as ours, but more stretched out, & is pointed in the end like a Pin, without having any other beard or tonge. They fasten not on their Bait, but the day before provide a quantitie of small Fish, as great as our little Bleaks, or Roches, which they find in great number on the Bankes and Sands, and keep them alive inclosed in little pursnets (made of the Thred of Cocos) with little Mashes, and let them hang in the Sea at the Sterne of their Barkes. When they come into the deepe Sea, they sow about their little Fishes, and let their Line hang downe. The great Fish seeing the little Fish, which is not frequent in the deepe Sea, runne together in great shoales, and by the same meanes they fasten them to their hookes, which they white and trim over; so that being a ravenous and foolish Fish, it takes the whited Hook, thinking it is a white little Fish. They doe nothing but lift their Line into their Boat, and the Fish falls off presently (being not strongly fastened) and then they put it into the Sea againe; thus they take a strange quantitie, so that in three or foure houres their Boates are in a manner full; and that which is remarkable, they go alwayes with full sayle. The Fish which they take thus they generally cal in their language Cobolly Masse, that is to say, the Blacke Fish, for they are all blacke.

They have another sort of fishing on their bankes, when the Moone is in the change, and when it is at the full, three daies eacha time. This they doe on Rafts made of the Wood, called Camdou. They have great Lines of fiftie or sixtie fathome pitched over. In the end they hang hookes wheron they fasten the baite as we doe, and thus take great quantitie of fish, one kinde very delicious, which they call the King of the Sea. They have all sorts of Nets and Toiles made of

Cotton twine, Weeles and other Instruments of fishing. Neere the Sea shoare, and where it is shallow, they passe their time, and take delight in fishing for small fish, like Pilchards with casting Nets. Twice in the Yueere at the Equinoctials, they make a generall fishing, a great number of persons assemble together in certaine indraughts of the Sea. The Sea at that time ariseth higher then all the times of the Yeere, and passeth the limits of other Tides, the Ebbe after the same proportion recoiles and retires, discovering theee Rockes and Shoalds, which at other times appeare not. In these places while the Sea is going out, they observe some fit corner, and set about it great stones, one upon another to a great height, so that it resembles a round Wall or Raveling. This inclosure hath forties paces in circuit or compasse: but the entrance is but two or three paces large. They gather together thritie or fortie men, and every one carrieth fiftie or sixie fathome of great coard of Cocos, where from fathome to fathome they tie a piece of the Barke of dried Cocos, to make it float on the water, as we use Corke: after, they tye them together, and stretch them out in a round upon the flats. It is strange, that all the fish which is within the coard, finding themselves taken, although there bee no other Nets nor Instruments, but the Coard which swimmeth on the water, but the fish fearing the Line and shadow of the Line; so that they dare not passe under to escape, but flye from the Line, thinking that it hath a Net underneath: The men goe all driving them to the inclsure of stone, drawing up the coard by little and little some in Boates, and some in the water (for upon these flats the Sea is shallow, and not above necke high for the most part lesse) so moderately drawing up the Line, the fish flye from it, and are locked up in the inclosure, so that in the end yhr Line being all drawne up, all the fishes enter in: and they speedily stop the entry with Faggots of boughes and leaves of Cocos, bound end to end, twentie or thirtie fathome, and compacted together about the greatnesse of a man, and so when the Sea is out, the fish remaine taken on the dry Land. They often take thus of all sorts ten and twelve thousand or more. This fishing they make but once in six monethes, upon every flat, and everytime continues five daies, and they change daily their divisions, and returne not often into the same place to fish in this manner, except at another Equinoctiall.

François Pyrard de Laval,
Hakluytus Posthumus or Purchas His Pilgrimes, *1905*

Dhoni Construction

The basic design of the traditional Maldivian seagoing vessel has changed little during recorded times. Timber from the coconut palm is still used, though these days some imported wood is also used to strengthen the structure of the hull. These resilient little craft are built by master carpenters using very few tools and no plans. Their skills are passed down from generation to generation within the same families in a genuine, living, oral tradition.

The boats are usually built inside coconut-thatched huts set at the water's edge. On some outer islands boat building supports the economy of the entire community. Boat carpenters are known as *kissaru vadin,* literally 'curved carpenters', and they command not only a high wage but a lot of respect within the community. Completing a *dhoni* can take two months as one of these craftsmen builds a 12-metre (40-foot) boat using only an axe, an adze to dress the wood, a drill made of a wooden hammer and an iron bit, a chisel, a mallet and a hammer.

The hull of the *dhoni* is called the *fashan,* and is made from planks of hard- wood taken from the base of the tree and fitted together with wooden nails so that the entire boat fits together like an interlocking jigsaw. This structure is secured by pounding brass or copper nails into the wooden slats. Fish oil is then smoothed over the hulls of the *mas dhoni* fishing boats, partly to aid its passage through the water and in the belief that it will ensure a good catch.

The Family

A well-defined division of labour exists within the Maldivian family, another age-old pattern that has yet to be widely disrupted by the onrush of progress. All outdoor work, the major part of which consists of fishing, is carried out by the men. The traditional function of women, aside from bearing children and doing the household chores, is to help process the fish and the breadfruit crop, to weave copra fibre and screw pine leaves into cloth and mats, and to collect cowrie shells from the beach.

Maldivian women are, however, accorded more freedom than in many other traditional Islamic societies. The practice of purdah was never wholly accepted, though veils were commonly used at different times in the past. The Maldivian national dress for women includes a snippet-like veil that continues to be worn to this day. Women are not expected to bring a dowry with them at marriage, neither are men required to pay more than a nominar bride price over and above the expenses of the wedding. Marriage does not diminish a woman's social status unduly, and as long as she adheres to Islamic codes no other rigid curbs are imposed, though individual sultans and qazis have held different views on the benefits of femal emancipation or women's full participation in society.

Things are not so well organized in law, which is not broad minded in the least. In court, a man's evidence is legally equivalent to that of three women. Marriage is usually conducted in the groom's house. Once he has the agreement of the girl he informs the local Islamic judge, the *qazi*, who confirms her acquiesence. The wedding itself is a minor affair, which the bride does not usually even attend, with just two witnesses to confirm the action of the *qazi*. The act of divorce, *vari*, like that of marriage, is carried out in accordance with religious law, the *sharia*. Thus a woman cannot terminate her marriage without her husband's consent, though a man can dump his wife merely by uttering the words *kaley thiya inee vari koffa,* or 'I divorce you', three times and then settling on her a reasonable amount of maintenance money. However, if a married man dies, his spouse is entitled to the proceeds of his estate.

Polygamy, another ancient practice, still exists, though is less common these days. The Islamic variation forbid any man more than three wives at any one time; and he must prove he is able to support all of them. Sultans traditionally always had three wives, but the institution of a harem, as occurred regularly in India, has never existed in the Maldives. The seventeenth-century French explorer, François Pyrard de Laval, relates an eyewitness account of a man who married and divorced 80 or 100 times during his lifetime. A contemporary Maldivian merchant, for instance, may still have two or three wives and live within his extended family, while a struggling fisherman on an outer island is probably thankful to have just one to support.

Fishing

Fishing is by a long chalk the most ubiquitous, and economically and socially the most important activity in the Maldives, a community affair throughout the atolls, particularly in the outer islands. The owner of a boat, the *masdhoni*, receives around 20-35 percent of the catch plus one fish per member of the crew in payment for prayers said for them while at sea, a practice that varies from island to island. The remainder is shared among the crew members, with the chief fisherman *(keolu)* getting the lion's share, followed by the chief bait fisherman, the *en keolu*.

The day starts very early as the bait fish have to be caught well before sunrise in the shallows of the lagoon. They are kept in a special compartment on board the dhoni so it looks to a foreign eye as if the boat is slowly flooding. Once at sea, the crew look out for circling flocks of birds which will show them where to find the tuna. They then throw the live bait overbaord and beat the water from the stern end of the boat to induce the tuna into a feeding frenzy. The fishermen swiftly and deftly set about hooking a big fish, landing it, then hooking another. Each man can catch up to 100 fish in an hour, literally picking them out of the water. The catch is normally sold on the beach. Fine tuna is

transported to Japan to be made into Sashimi. Back on shore the village awaits
the boats' return with anticipation. Even suppliers on the island providing sails
and hooks will be paid in kind rather than cash.

Entertainment and Games

In the age before television, diversions and amusements were generated from
within society as an expression of their togetherness, usually through movement or music. With the strictures of Islam firmly observed in the Maldives,
it is usually only the men who get to dance, such behaviour being considered
most unseemly for girls who have passed puberty ('hanging loose' is definitely
something that only men should do). Dances are usually performed to celebrate
special occasions and are ritualized around specific ceremonies and rites of
passage like Malé circumcision. Visitors will probably be shown a local
'cultural performance' at their resort, performed either by a travelling troupe
of professional dancers or more likely by the resort's kitchen staff after hours.

The best known traditional Maldivian dance is *bodu beri*, thought to have
been brought to the Maldives by African settlers as long ago as the 12th-century.
The musical instruments are usually a trio of coconut-wood drums lashed tautly
with the hide of a stingray, a small bell, and an *onugadu*, a piece of bamboo
in which notches have been cut to produce an eerie, gamelan-like sound. The
band is accompanied by about 15 *lungi*-clad Malé dancers who start gyrating in
a very slow, swaying rhythm, throwing their arms about and gradually becoming
progressively wilder and more frantic as they continue late into the night.
One type of *bodu* called the *tara* was recently banned because frenzied dancers
climaxed the performance by repeatedly bashing their heads with spiked clubs
until their blood ran. An Indian-style *bandiyya jehun*, a gentler, harvest or
fertility dance performed by very young women who beat metallic water pots
in time to an accompanying song. *Gaa odi lava* is a dance traditionally performed before the sultan as an expression of gratitude for his benevolence.
The dancers move around a box that in the old days held the sultan's gift of
money. As with most Maldivian dances, it starts slowly but the tempo increases
as it progresses.

The songs accompanying these dances are sung in a mixture of Arabic and
Divehi, while some words apparently derive from languages from central Africa.
The oldest form of folk music is known as *thaara*, said to have been introduced
by the Persians and the Arabs in the seventeenth-century. Its chanted lyrics are
uttered in Arabic and accompanied by a multi drum rhythm section of great
virtuosity. *Raivaru* is an old type of poetry few can understand today, intoned
in a dragging, repetitive tune often accompanied by a slow dance. The senti-
ments expressed are very often in code language and can be difficult even for
Maldivians to decipher.

Maldivians are not much into games. One you might see is known as *bai bala*, a wrestling sport in which a single player enters a ring and attempts to touch members of the opposite team. If he can escape without being helped out of the ring then all those whom he has touched are eliminated. *Mandi* is a traditional sport in which a small stick is propelled by players with slightly longer sticks. Opponents are required to catch it without letting it drop to the ground, a bit like a stick version of the 'hakky-sack' game played in Vietnam and certain English schools with a small hide-covered ball. A popular children's game is *gandu filla*. Here a player has to be identified by the opposite team while the other members of his team usually remain hidden, a bit like hide-and-seek with a detective element tagged on. A variation of chess exists but with slightly modified rules. The traditional Arabic game of *carrom*, a bit like cueless billards, is also played, plus a board game called *ovvalu* which uses money cowries placed in little dips in board, a good teaching aid to get children to count.

If you develop a taste for Maldivian music, or if you want to purchase a cassette as a curiosity to give to your friends, you can find tapes of famous Maldivian love songs and *bodu beri* music in several music stores in Malé. The John Lennon of the Maldives is called Hassan Fulu. But on the whole, popular culture doesn't reach much beyond imported music and the ubiquitous Hindi movies from Bombay. Only one film has ever been made locally in the entire history of the country, a Maldivian-Egyptian co-production called *'Youssef and Zeinab'* filmed in 1986. The plot centres, not surprisingly, on an Egyptian man visiting the Maldives to teach English who falls in love with a local Maldivian girl. There are no plans for a sequel.

Crafts

Indigenous crafts are thin on the ground. The best *kunaar,* mats made from leaves of the screw pine, are said to be dyed, woven, and hand-printed on Gaddu in Gaafu-Dhaalu Atoll. The finest lacquerwork is reputed to originate from Thuludu in Baa Atoll. Lengths of traditional *feyli* cloth are also woven in Baa. Carved wooden models of *dhonis* often come from islands in North Maalhosmadulu Atoll. Modern gold jewellery is made in Ribudhu, silver in Hulhudheli, both of them islands in South Nilandhe Atoll. Black coral and mother-of-pearl may likely come from Fadipolu in Lhaviyani Atoll. Fish bones decorated with black coral or mother-of-pearl are also made by local artisans, though the red coral made in Dhaal Atoll is imported from China. (Note. Avoid buying black coral products, as it is endangered worldwide, and cannot be legally imported into many countries.)

Architecture

On the outer islands, untouched by developments in Malé whose modern
houses have little charm, you can still see the unique style of traditional
Maldivian architecture which makes ingenious use of natural fibres and
materials. Coral serves as both bricks and mortar; burned slowly in deep
pits, it yields a powerful lime cement. Houses are constructed almost
entirely of coral slates and *cadjan* (coconut leaf-thatched roofs) and en-
closed by a coral wall around a garden, usually above its own water well.
These walls are about head height to ensure some privacy since the enclo-
sure serves as a traditional Maldivian open-air bathroom. Some tourist
resorts have adopted this design in their huts; few experiences can be more
pleasant than lying in an open-air bath raised above the coral sand, surrounded by fragrant frangipani and screw pine bushes yet privately open to
the sky. Powdered coral sand is used to surface the floors and the surrounding garden area, and most households have their own well sunk to a depth
of about two metres (six feet) to tap the rain-filled—and these days invari-
ably brackish—wate rtable under most islands. Water is drawn from this
gilfi with the aid of a long wooden pole armed at its end with a large ladle
called a *dhaani*.

One of the pleasing aspects of the Maldives is that everything is kept so
spotlessly clean. Coral paths are brushed each day and many everyday
objects are made out of natural rather than man-made materials. Coconut
husks are turned into coir for matting; screw pine husks are woven and
hand-printed into aesthetic decorations called *tundu kuna,* while the leaves
are turned into baskets. Special *cadjan* mats are made from large coconut
leaves woven together with coir rope to form roof-thatching material. Wood
is very scarce in the Maldives so houses are quite devoid of it. Indeed it is
so precious there is a special market in Malé for imported fire wood.

Rooms are often small, but the furnishings are neat and simple. A flat
bench serves as a rudimentary bed at night and a place to sit during the day.
Tucked under the bed is usually a heavy wooden chest where the family's
worldly goods and treasures are stored. The lack of furniture is really
unimportant as families spend most of their time outside on the veranda,
the social focus of the home, where they can sit under the shade of a leafy
breadfruit tree as protection against the relentless sun. It is usual to find an
undoali strung up, a large wooden swing in which to idle away the hours.
There are also hammock-style chairs known as *joali* made from wood
and coir rope. Domestic craftsmen are known as *ted ui vadin*, and generally
every inhabited island has one who turns out chests, tables, and swings.

Modern life

Many young Maldivians are eager to taste the outside world, though this desire for liberty is not encouraged by the government which operates what amounts to a bonded labour scheme so that every Maldivian going overseas to study has to dedicate extra years on his return to his already statutory period of government service—a move that tends to dampen the brightest and focus restless minds inwards. Nevertheless, the outside world is spreading its tentacles farther and farther, year by year, despite the careful segregation of tourists from as many of the native population as possible. In the past the Maldives was a mecca in its own right for Indians seeking cheap electronic goods to take back to their homeland. Today most Indians prefer to go to Singapore to pick up their cheap electronic goods to smuggle past the abnormally alert customs officials back home. Malé's shops instead display items coveted by the growing Maldivian middle class, including many objects whose usefulness is of doubtful veracity and dubious taste.

Crime and Punishment

The Maldives follows a moderate version of the Islamic legal code, the *sharia*, which does not compel women to wear the *chador*, stone adulterers, or chop off the hands of thieves. It has, however, refined its own form of an ancient punishment: banishment to a remote island, usually for eight months, or sometimes for one or two years. This cuts off the prisoners from all family ties. While at first

encountering a hostile reaction from local inhabitants and being treated as pariahs, they are later often accepted in their cuckoo community, a curiously effective form of social rehabilitation. The system was introduced by the Maldivian royal family as means of controlling troublesome rivals. African slaves, thought to have been brought back from the *Hajj* pilgrimage to Mecca, were often very rebellious and found themselves consigned to Felidhu in Ari Atoll.

Witch Doctors

Superstition still rules the lives of many Maldive islanders. Evil spirits like the *jinni*, and the amorphous *dhevi*, are thought to come from the sea, land, and sky. Their machinations can account for everything that cannot be explained by either religion or education.

Historians say these beliefs arose long before the arrival of Islam in the Maldives, at a time when its people felt themselves simultaneously at one and at the mercy of the primordial natural forces surrounding them in their island world. To please and appease the forces of nature, these spirits had to be worshipped. According to an ancient Maldivian myth, one evil spirit called the *Rannamaari* was a particularly truculent *jinni* which several centuries ago required the regular sacrifice of virgins. Adherents catalogue more than 50 categories of spirit which require a variety of incarnations. One spirit resembles a horse with a light coming from its forehead, another an old woman, a third a shadow that can appear in the shape of a human being, or a grey monkey, or with an elephant's trunk, as a tortoise, or covered in sparks of fire, or as a seven-headed woman. Some spirits induce epilepsy, madness, or death. Beneficent ones can repair rotten teeth, but most prefer to suck blood from human veins, make dhonis run aground, or sexually molest women.

The only weapon to combat the evil *jinnis* are the *fandita* —the name literally means 'to cast out'—which are the spells and lotions concocted by the local *hakeem* or witchdoctor, a village man who acts as a combination of exorcist, conjurer, herbalist, and astrologer. He becomes qualified to practise the art of *fandita* only after passing an arcane examination, mysterious to all noninitiates. The *hakeem* is often called upon when illness strikes, if a woman fails to conceive, or if the fishing catch is consistently poor. He might cast a curing spell by writing phrases from the Koran on strips of paper, sticking or tying them to the patient while reciting the sayings out loud. Another method is to write them in ink on a plate which is then filled with water and given to the patient to drink. Traditional Maldivian medicine, known as *divei bais,* is prepared by the *hakeem* from local and imported herbs and is remarkably similar to the traditional herbal medicines of the Orient.

Other concoctions include *isitri*, a love potion used by unrequited lovers to enhance their powers of attraction (its antidote, *varitoli* is used to break up marriages). Considering the frequency of divorce in the Maldives this does not appear to be used very often, but according to a *hakeem* I spoke to the consequences of an *istiri* or *varitoli* that backfires can be disastrous. Clairvoyance is known as *faalu* and is used both to predict the future and locate missing objects, or even to obtain the description of a person suspected of committing an offence.

Fandita charms are used primarily to heal or to encourage the environment to behave more favourably, like providing better fishing catches. However, the practice of *sihuru*, Maldivian sorcery and black magic, can land an advocate in very deep trouble and even a period of banishment from society to a remote island. Other forms of good magic exist, such as *naduru*, a sacred vow pledged to perform a good deed if and when the desired preconditions are fulfilled. This might involve anything from a simple to an elaborate sacrifice, or the giving of alms. When a child becomes sick, bananas or *naduru foli*, a wafer-thin pancake equal to the weight of the child, are sometimes distributed.

Banishment is meted out today for a range of offences, mainly religious ones. These include the secret tippling of alcohol, premarital sex, stealing, and wilful breaking of the Ramadan fast. Since the community is so small there is hardly any privacy and infractions are hard to hide and easily unmasked. Lashings are also given to lesser offenders by those described to me by the chief judge in Malé as 'certain trained people'. These chastisements take place in the capital's police station with an instrument that looks like a long cook's ladle topped by an oblong handle which delivers a hearty thwack without drawing blood. The president has the final say as to whether a person should be banished or merely lashed. Otherwise it is up to a clutch of *qazis*, the judges that sit in the jury-free Islamic court. They obviously have a lot to do despite the Maldivians' generally placid nature and easy-going life style. Every inhabited island has a court, and Malé has eight! Despite this, the country doesn't even have a prison to hold its criminal offenders, though one island is in effect a high-security prison where the leaders of the 1988 coup attempt are serving out their life banishment.

In recent times, an increasing number of citizens have been banished for embezzlement and fraud, a knock-on effect of the influx of new wealth as Maldivians aspire to become richer. Malé is hardly New York, though; there hasn't been a case of murder, other than one committed by a foreigner, since 1953. And the attorney-general thinks that crime can be all but eradicated by promoting volleyball, cricket and other sports and encouraging people to eat more fish.

The etiquette of conviction is as bizarre as the punishments that the guilty receive. Suspects have to be personally accused in a courtroom confrontation, something completely alien to most western countries. Unmarried lovers or adulterers have to be confronted by no less than four witnesses, which would seem to leave the door wide open to promiscuity (or tightly bolted, depending on your point of view). It is considered very bad form to accuse someone with only circumstantial evidence to back up the claim.

The catalogue of potential crimes makes interesting reading. Saying bad things about the president or his family, or questioning the political order of the Maldives (which amounts to the same thing), are high on the list. This effectively curbs freedom of speech and people are very wary of getting into any kind of political discussion or expressing their opinions openly, even in private. Nor should the Prophet's name be taken in vain. Members of parliament cannot be prosecuted, however, for expressing their thoughts because what is said in the *maljis*, is considered confidential.

Around 600 people are currently banished, some 250 of whom are thought to be under house arrest as political prisoners. Prominent political offenders are sent to Dhoonidhoo, a small island just north of Malé where they can be billeted in the former residence of the British governor. In general, women suffer the worst as banishment is synomymous with the loss of social grace. In Maldivian

terms, one becomes a scarlet women and an easy target for tom-catting village men. The experience can be ameliorated, though, for families often make arrangements for banished relatives to be fed and lodged by an island family. Wealthier criminals are free to make even more comfortable arrangements.

Several westerners have suffered this unusual incarceration, being set down on a sparsely populated or uninhabitated island with only a few coconut palms and some government-supplied fish hooks to stave off starvation. One was an American college student who tried to sell hashish to the police chief's son. The islanders, strict Muslims all, demanded he take refuge in the headman's house every time a native woman approached the tree under which he lived. A German who strangled his French girlfriend in 1976 fared better. He grew so fond of his personal exile on Fuludu island in Raa Atoll that he kicked drugs and alcohol, according to local police. When the German ambassador flew in from Sri Lanka to tell him he could be deported back to Germany to complete his sentence his answer was 'No thanks, I like it better here'. He has since converted to Islam and married a local woman.

The Maldives must be the only tourist destination in the world that treats its criminal elements the same as it does its high-paying visitors! Banishment has become so popular that at least three other Germans and a Swede have demanded to be punished for minor drug offenses by being exiled in paradise. This method of visa extension is not recommended as the government favours the simpler solution of deporting troublesome aliens.

Signs and Symbols

The national flag of the Maldives is a green rectangle, representing the universal colour of Islam, with a red border, which is the blood of the nation in sacrifice, with a white crescent in the centre, which is the symbol of the faith. The national emblem is a bit more prosaic; the ubiquitous coconut palm, crescent and star and two crisscrossed national flags. The national tree is, of course, the coconut palm, and the national flower is the pink rose. Of the two international tests of administrative credibility—the size of a country's postage stamps and the dimensions of its entry visa, the Maldives scores low marks for the former and high marks— i e. it has a small entry stamp—for the latter.

Malé

The tiny, saucer-shaped island capital of the Maldives is rarely more than a
port of entry (and for most visitors, not even that). Malé—pronounced 'Mah-
lee'—may have the distinction of being the largest island in the archipelago,
but it is hardly a metropolis. Even the government suggests politely that you
go straight to your resort without delaying here. To a visitor's eye this administrative hamlet of coral-stone houses and sandy streets appears in a state of
continual siesta. Squat, tannin-skinned fishermen wearing petticoat *lungis*
shuffle through the coral dust down the main street with slippery tuna draped
over their shoulders like gunny bags. The women leave a trace of coconut oil
in the air as they waft past in long nylon or cotton dresses which cover their
bodies in the burqa fashion with snippet-like veils, a relic from a brief period
under Portuguese rule.

Taxi drivers blast out strains of 'Abba', the saccharine-sweet Swedish pop
group, into the empty, pavement-less streets. Meanwhile, the capital's cruisers
ride the potholes high up in pick-up trucks on the look out for unwary jay-
walkers (who commit an offence by not crossing at designated places). The
local boys try to show off their manhood by collecting scars from motorbike
pile-ups, which are dainty affairs at the best of times because there's a 25 kph
(15 mph) speed limit on the sand-blown main street. There are only 494
registered motor vehicles anyway, too few for the Maldivians to have got
around to introducing car insurance yet or to drop the need to register your
bicycle with the authorities. When it rains the town turns to a pond, then an
unimaginable coral slush, but then the water drains away in minutes leaving
just a few dried rivulets to show its passing.

The smell of fish permeates everywhere. The waterfront is barely visited
apart from a flurry of activity after the fishing catch is landed in the early
hours of the morning. Indian Hindi film music wafts out of single-storey
shopfronts selling imported Singaporean polyesters and thongs. Locals seem
to have a fetish for imported lacy items, and plastic goods have the gleam of
gold for young Maldivians. The kids hang out in two cafés called 'Quench'
and 'Downtown', opposite each other on Mijheedhee Magu. The town's single
neon sign is in Hindi, in sharp contrast to the Maldivian *thaana* script.

A tangible lethargy hangs in the air with the embankment's salty wafts.
Along the waterfront wild-eyed fishermen with stained gums lurk in tea shops
with names like 'Queen of the Night' and 'Beach Cafe' chewing betel.
wrapped in a leaf with coral lime and a stick of clove. Or they smoke *bidis*
made of a single leaf of tobacco wrapped in old newspaper, of formidable
strength and for all the world looking like huge reefers. An advertisement
for an upcoming civic attraction listed 'Fairy Cocktails' at the local high
school gym.

For the tiny group of Western expats, Malé is a one-bar (in the Nasandhura Palace Hotel) town, a marooned city of caged birds and shuffling noises where you are always bumping into people. It has an air of decline that hasn't yet reached the genteel. The museum looks like a gardener's shed sheltering under shady mangosteen trees and the minaret of the main mosque, its first exhibit a bullet-ridden Honda 125 from the last coup attempt in 1988. It also used to have an impressive collection of pre-Buddhist statues dug up in the islands by Thor Heyerdahl, but most of them got thrown out to make way for a state visit by the Malaysian prime minister some years ago.

I met the attorney general, a rather avuncular man who had a theory that crime could be significantly reduced by getting people to eat large amounts of fish. Since no Maldivians have murdered each other for several decades, maybe he has a point. As the sun declines, evening joggers—members of the National Security Force not currently on duty—make a circuit of the island. Usually they stand, armed with automatic rifles, in front of the President's palace and the parliament building, the Majlis, with its peppermint colours and pastel tiles.

The *muezzin's* mournful cry blares out across the flat roofs from tinny loudspeakers, organizing the last of the day's prayers for the Sunni faithful in the 40 or so mosques around the capital. Afterwards, the liveliest part of town is the evening fish market, overspilling with old detergent bottles filled with fish paste. It starts at six in the morning and finishes about nine in the evening, around the point of darkness. At dusk it fills up with the day's catch, with the largest fish, a swordfish, lying pellucid on a platter for inspection. Other foods grown in the Maldives include sweet potato, cassava, taro, and the occasional cucumbers, spinach, sorghum, red onions, ridge gourds and bitter gourds, cabbages and chillies, all from the south. If you're lucky you may find watermelons from far-off Thuddhu in Ari Atoll, or guavas, jujubes, custard and wood apples, or even sapodillas.

The kids are congregating in the milk shake bars again, concrete huts nestling under the arches of the football stadium on the main street, part of the big renovation made in the 1970s before the tourist boom took off. With electricity shortages, fridges and airconditioners do not always work. Water can be in short supply also. A desalination plant built in 1988 supplies only 200 cubic meters (44,000 gallons) daily, a fraction of the town's needs. Malé used to have some 6,000 wells bored into the freshwater water table that reached down 20 metres (66 feet) years ago, or at least it did in 1921 when the census put the population at 6,127. With almost 100 times that number 70 years later, the average depth of the watertable is only about 1.2 metres (3.6 feet), shallower than the trenches in the road. Coastal sea defences will keep out freak storm waves, but the freshwater level must rise as the sea level rises so that Malé and all the Maldivian islands appear doomed to eventual extinction.

Orientation

It is quite possible to walk from one end of Malé to the other in 20 minutes, so finding your way around the island is very straightforward. You'll need your map to navigate Malé's streets and alleys, however, since many are either in Divehi script or unmarked. It's useful to know that *magu* is the Maldivian word for a wide, unpaved coral street, *goalhi* is a narrow alley, and a *higun* is a slightly longer and wider one.

The main centre of activity is Marine Drive, the harbour front strip that wraps itself halfway around the island from the north. The other principal streets are the north-south Chandani Magu and Majidi Magu which divides it east to west. The capital is divided into four districts—Maafannu, Machangolhi, Henveiru, and Galohu—though you cannot notice much difference. Maafannu covers the northwestern end of the island from the Singapore bazaar area of Chandani Magu; it encloses the presidential residence, some of the foreign embassies, and many of Malé's guesthouses. Machangolhi runs east-west across the middle of the island and contains Malé's popular shopping strip, Majidi Magu. Galohu is a crowded maze of coral-stone houses in the southeastern end of Malé, where you can see how most residents live. Henveiru in the north-eastern pocket of Malé encloses Ameer Ahmed Magu where wealthier Maldivians live in slightly more elaborate villas on Marine Drive overlooking the harbour. The reclaimed land is largely to the south, which is where the industrial activity, such as it is, is concentrated. The fishing and cargo port is to the west of Chandani Magu; the tourist and yacht harbour to the east

The Islamic Centre

The huge, gold-domed, three-storey Islamic Centre, the island's most famous and most vivid architectural landmark with its 133 minarets, was declared open by President Ghayoom in 1984. It houses an Islamic library, a conference hall, and classrooms where a number of activities are conducted. Most important is the centrepiece **Grand Mosque**, named after Sultan Muhammad Thakurufaanu Al A'zam, which can shelter over 5,000 people. Its main prayer hall displays beautiful woodcarvings and Arabic calligraphy created by Maldivian craftsmen; four huge chandeliers and purpose-woven carpets add a glossy touch.

Hukuru Miskiiy—The Friday Mosque

The Friday Mosque was built in 1656 during the reign of Sultan Ibrahim Iskandhar and stands on the site of the very first mosque in Malé. The exterior is built from coral stones fitted together along grooves, not with masonry. The interior is intricately carved with Arabic writings and woocarvings in coconut, teak, sandalwood and mahogany relating the conversion of the Maldives to Islam. Coral carvings showing geometrical designs and local flora are quite

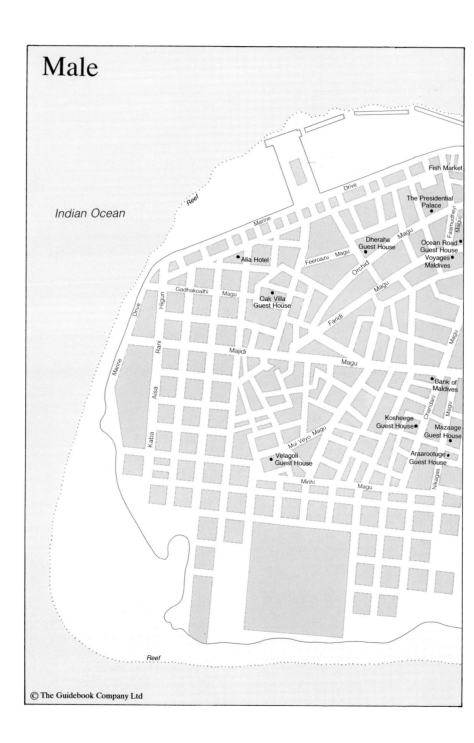

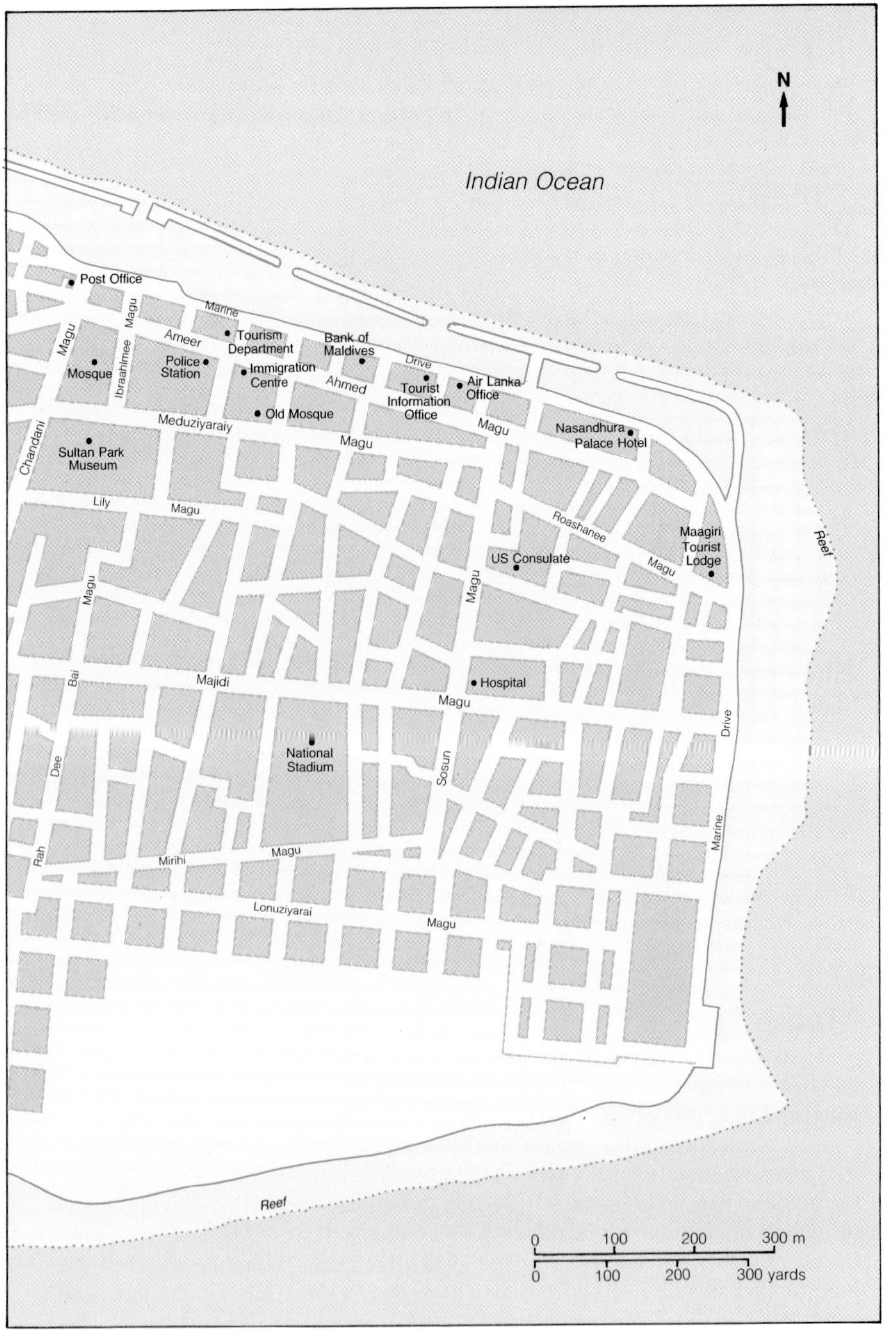

N

Indian Ocean

Post Office

Marine

Magu

Magu

Ameer

Ibraahimee Magu

Tourism
Department

Bank of
Maldives

Drive

Mosque

Police
Station

Immigration
Centre

Ahmed

Tourist
Information
Office

Air Lanka
Office

Chandani

Meduziyaraiy

Old Mosque

Magu

Magu

Nasandhura
Palace Hotel

Sultan Park
Museum

Roashanee

Maagiri
Tourist
Lodge

Lily

Magu

US Consulate

Magu

Reef

Magu

Magu

Bai

Majidi

Hospital

Magu

Dee

National
Stadium

Sosun

Drive

Rah

Mirihi

Magu

Marine

Lonuziyarai

Magu

Reef

| 0 | 100 | 200 | 300 m |

| 0 | 100 | 200 | 300 yards |

unusual. Inside, the mosque has three *dhaalas*, raised platforms placed on all sides except the west. Inscriptions in Arabic and *dhives akuru* on the walls spell out duties of the imam. Twelve lacquered domes in the roof are covered with floral designs in bright colours of red, blue, green, and gold.

Outside there are four wells within the compound walls for ritual ablutions. The sundial is only about 70 years old and was used to calculate the five times of daily prayer. In a bid to preserve the mosque, the thatched roof at the western end was covered with corrugated iron in 1912, and aluminium in 1964, to prevent the sun's rays falling directly on the mosque, though this has somewhat marred the historic beauty of the building. The *munnaaru* minaret was erected in 1668 after the then sultan made the *hajj* pilgrimage to Mecca; it was renewed early this century with iron and copper bindings on the outside replacing the old rope ones. Loudspeakers for the *mudhim*, the *muezzins*'s call to prayer, were installed in 1964 but are not used today.

The compound also includes a number of ancient tombstones, erected in memory of past kings, noblemen, and heroes, including Sultan Ibrahim Iskander I who repulsed the Portuguese raid of 1649. The last sultan buried here was Sheik Ibrahim Rushdy, some 30 years ago. The pointed stones indicate graves of men, the round ones, women's graves.

Eid Miskiiy

Malé's second-largest mosque is in the western part of the town. It was built in 1815 on the site of an earlier one using a design borrowed from the Friday Mosque.

Medhu Ziyaarath

Opposite the Friday Mosque is the Medhu Ziyaarath, a shrine in memorial to Abul Barakaath-Al Barbarie, revered as the man who promoted the conversion of the Maldives to Islam in 1153. The white flag flown each Friday is a weekly commemoration of this heavily mythologized figure.

Mulee-Aage—The Presidential Palace

This palace was built by Sultan Shamshuddin III in about 1913 for his son and heir, Al Ameer Hassan Izzaiyadheen. In 1936 he and his son were banished and their property forfeited to the government. It became the chief council house during the Second World War and location of the archipelago's first *maakoani* radio, which was used to listen to wartime broadcasts. When the republic was proclaimed in 1953, the palace became the president's official residence and famous for its nursery of rare plants. It was also the chief guesthouse, probably the only place where Queen Elizabeth II and the leader of the Palestinian Liberation Organization, Yasser Arafat, have slept in the same bed, albeit at different times. The site was historically the family home of the Huravee family, starting with Hassan Maniffaar, who expelled the Malabari invaders in the fifteenth-century. The current building was designed by Sinhalese and Maldivian architects and reflects a colonial rather than an indigenous or Islamic influence. This doesn't explain the garish pastel tiles on the outside which certainly look like a local fetish and can hardly be blamed on British colonialism. Subsequent governments used the palace to house state offices and made alterations to the official residence. In 1953, when the country became a republic for the second time, Muleeaage became the presidential palace.

Sultan Park Museum

The museum in the Sultan's Park used to be part of the old Royal Palace. It was seen by the French exile François Pyrard de Laval in the early seventeenth-century but was destroyed by a Malabari invasion in 1752. The rest was destroyed in the 1960s, as the government at the time did not appreciate its historical value. It embodies, in its current incarnation, all that is endearing and infuriating about the Maldives. The building resembles a gardener's shed watched over by a covey of old men who make it obvious they don't really like to be disturbed. Opened in 1952, the whole place is permeated with an air of decrepitude and vagueness, as if nobody can quite sort it all out.

The cannon outside is a legacy of the Portuguese occupation that ended in 1573 (others can be seen in different places along Malé's waterfront, not quite cleared away and absorbed into the landscape). Relics from Thor Heyerdahl's expedition lie in a corner, as yet unlabelled, in a disorganized rubble of sandstone and coral. Most were found in the southernmost islands, including Ari Atoll, and all date prior to the Maldives' twelfth-century conversion to Islam, which perhaps explains their state of semibenign neglect. The Buddha head from Kurendhu in Lhaviyani Atoll was found in 1962. Pride of place goes to the three-metre-high (ten feet) head from Thudhu. Mundu island has provided some carved lions and a monkey's head.

The rest of the museum is chock-a-block with odds and ends. A random selection gives the flavour of the collection, bizarre yet curiously fascinating: the decrepit first printing press sent to the Maldives; palanquins used by the last sultan in 1932; a photograph of the moon by Neil Armstrong; and an old sandglass egg timer. One of my favourites is a newspaper cutting by an early travel writer, one C W Rossett, from a London illustrated magazine *The Graphic,* dated 1886 and showing a plump girl idling in a swinging chair with the caption 'this the chief amusement of Maldives women.' Elsewhere, the antiquarian will be pleased by examples of the old script *dhives akuru* engraved on a wooden plank and dating from the thirteenth-century, and old coins dating from 1620 showing the progression from coins shaped like little pins instead of being round to recognizable circular money. At the modern end there's a vast range of mouldering ceremonial attire, embroidered coats that belonged to the sultans' womenfolk, ghoulish sepia photographs, silver ornaments, letters from colonial visitors, eighteenth-century turbans, lacquer trays used for a sultan's special holiday food, tin drum-holders used to sound imperial gongs, knifes and sundry seals, prayer carpets, broken model boats, and rickety umbrellas made of cotton and used to shade the sun's rays from the sultan's eyes. More poignant are the two bullet-ridden motorbikes on which a lancecorporal in the security forces was killed in the brief crossfire during the last coup attempt. A sarong used by the nation's saviour, Thakurafaanu, is the most valuable item, and the oldest. The museum is open 9–11.30 am, then from 3–5.40 pm, entry Rf5.

Bihuroazu Kamanaa Miskiiy

The tomb of Mohammed Thakurufaanu, the Maldivian hero who defeated the occupying Portuguese and restored the country's independence, lies in the compound of this mosque. He died in 1585.

Ali Rasgefaanu Ziyaarath

Although Sultan Ali VI, popularly known as Ali Rasgefaanu, ruled the country for only two and a half months, his place in Maldivian history is secure as one of the country's greatest heroes. He died in 1558 while defending the homeland from Portuguese mercenaries. The tombstone marks the exact spot in the sea where the sultan fell after being hit by an enemy arrow. Then it stood in knee-deep water, but recent reclamation has brought the memorial site onto dry land.

Malé Directory

Hotels and Guesthouses

Do not fall into the trap of looking for a place to stay during the peak season, without booking well in advance, as there is so little space it will use up a lot of the time you could be spending on the beach or on a boat. The main hotels in Malé are often block-booked by aid agencies for staffers working on development projects in the Maldives. The two main areas in which to look for accommodation are to the left of the main jetty as you arrive on Marine Drive, and in the central area. Expect to pay a lot for what you get if you want anything above the most basic room for the night. Food is generally pretty poor.

Expensive

Nasandhura Palace Hotel, Marine Drive. Tel. 32-3380, 2360; fax. 32-4300; tlx. 66091 POLYCOM MF. The marine-front location is convenient for late-night arrivals or early morning departures to and from the airport. A spartan two-storey block which is far from palatial, but it is the best hotel in Malé. The restaurant has an à la carte menu. The bar is a favourite with Malé's tiny expatriate community who linger here virtually all day to down Heineken and Singapore Lion beer and evening cocktails, an oasis in an otherwise alcohol-free Malé. Airconditioned rooms, s/d $55–75 including breakfast.

Alia Hotel, 32 Marine Drive. Tel. 32-2080, 3445, 2935; tlx. 77032 HOTALIA MF (airconditioned rooms, s/d $52–64; with fans).

Sosunge, Sosun Magu. Tel. 32-3025, 3026; tlx. 66019 TOURISM MF. Was run as a government guesthouse before renovation.

Moderate

Bamboo, tel. 32–3241.	Maagiri Tourist Lodge, tel. 32–2576.
Buruneege, tel. 32-4140.	Gaadhoo, tel. 32-3222.
Lifshaam, tel. 32-5386.	Meedhu, tel. 32-2534.
Sakeena Menzil, tel. 32-3281	Sony, tel. 32-3249.

At the west end of Malé in Maafannu

Malé Tour Inn Guesthouse, tel. 32–3018.

Shaheed Ali Hingun. tel. 32-6220.

Kaimoo, tel. 32-3241.

Mermaid Inn, tel. 32-3329.

Velagali, tel. 32-2267.

Ever Pink, tel. 32–4751.

Fehividhuvaruge, tel. 32–4470.

Maafaru, tel. 32-2220.

Ocean Reed, tel. 32-3311.

At the the southern end, in Galolhu

Greenlin, tel. 32-2279

Tetra, tel. 32-3305.

Selvio, tel. 32-4671

In the central area of Machchangolhi

Araarootuge Guesthouse, tel. 32–2661.

Camelia, tel. 32–4642.

Kosheege, tel. 32-3585.

Nivikoa, tel. 32-2942.

Andaapoolge, tel. 32–2173.

Dawn Shine, tel. 32-5211.

Mazaage, tel. 32-4669.

Thaalin, tel. 32-4036.

Restaurants

Seagull Cafe House, Bageechage Fareedhee Magu. Open 9.30 am to 10.30 pm Saturday–Thursday, Fridays after 12.30 pm. The best food in town. Relaxed atmosphere with sand underfoot and scrabbling ants. Fresh fruit, Italian-style ice cream. Kurumba Surprise—fresh coconut stuffed with ice cream, topped with biscuit and fruit. Lavazza coffee for expresso and cappuchino, sandwiches, frappes, milkshake; pasta, lobster, grilled fish.

Cowrie Currency

The tiny cowrie shell turned the Maldives into a focus of international activity long before tourists were ever invented. The shell of *Cypraea moneta,* the money cowrie, was used in the lands bordering the Indian Ocean as a currency for over 3,000 years, and at least until the end of the seventeenth century. The archipelago served as a kind of mint for the entire region, a fact witnessed by Arab merchants 1,000 years ago as they began their expansion southwards in a bid to take over these lucrative trade routes. The legendary traveller, Ibn Battuta, visited the Maldives in 1343 and noted how the islanders cultivated cowries by putting palm leaves on the water's surface so that the molluscs would attach themselves. Then they dragged the leaves ashore and buried them in pits along the beach, so that the flesh would rot and leave only the bleached shells. He relates how the Maldivians sold them to Yemeni traders to serve as ballast, to Bengalis for rice, and to West Africans (by way of Amsterdam) at an exchange rate on a par with gold.

A Chinese chronicler who came with Cheng Ho's expedition to the Indian Ocean in 1433 tells how the cowries circulated in Bengal and Thailand. The Portuguese navigator, Vasco da Gama, found them when he came at the turn of the fifteenth-century and tried to wrest the monopoly away from the Arabs. The shipwrecked Frenchman, François Pyrard de Laval, witnessed 40 ships leaving fully laden in 1611. Instances of use in China, central Finland, and East Africa show how far the trade routes went.

The cowries succumbed to two influences at about the same time: marauding Portuguese adventurers who disrupted the apparently efficient open-port system that prevailed in nearby Calicut and elsewhere in the region, and the arrival of the first coins around 1600 which put paid to the wild fluctuations in the cowries' value depending on the particular region in which it was traded. As recently as 90 years ago, the historian H.C.P. Bell recounts that men on Isdu had to pay the sultan a tax

Snax, Majeedhee Magu. Noon-midnight. Malé's first fast-food outlet complete with chilly airconditioning (evenings only). Offerings include 'Kentucky Fried Chicken' and 'Big Mac burgers', not to mention black forest gateaux from a list of 78 items. Tel. 32-3241.

Bamboo, near the Customs Building. Currently a guesthouse charging $35 night. Its French owner serves French, Creole, and Italian food. Tel. 32–3241.

Beach Cafe, downtown at intersection of Madji Magu and Marine Drive. Open 9 am to 1 am. Maldivian and European style, milkshakes and snacks, including the exotic *dhonkeyo kajuru* made of deep-fried bananas.

Queen of the Night, Marine Drive, and **The Tea Shop**, Ameer Ahmed Magu.

of 18,000 cowries annually for themselves and a wife.

Almost all of our knowldge of Maldivian history comes from a chronicle called the Ta'rikh, compiled by the scholar Hasan Taj al-Din. This Arabic manuscript relates the story from the conversion of the first sultan, al-Malik al-'Adil Muhammad, up to the mid-nineteenth century, almost 700 years of history. A complete copy was presented to the British in Colombo and then lost, though the monograph by H.C.P. Bell, a former British Commissioner who first visited the islands in 1879, shows that he had seen it. Several versions written at other times have been found by a Japanese scholar in Malé.

Mention of the Maldives is made in sixth-century Alexandrian chronicles which placed it as one of the 1,370 islands adjacent to the largest of all islands, Taprobane, which we now call India. Arabic and Persian words entered the language, evidence of cross-fertilization from the north, as Tamil words are from the east. Other ancient scripts relate evidence of Maldivian participation in the Hajj pilgrimage to Mecca, and of the migration and exchange of reformist sufis and mullahs across the Indian Ocean. It is mentioned extensively in the travel books of Ibn Battuta, and a host of other Arabic travellers like al-Biruni, al-Idrisi, al-Dimashqi, and Ibn Majid.

It appears clear that the first recorded king of the Maldives was known as Prince Koimala who came to the country with his wife, the daughter of the king of Sri Lanka, in the early twelfth century. Contemporary Chinese chronicles call the area 'Three thousand weak waters', a reference dating back to the fifth century BC. It appears that the Maldives' conversion to Islam took place over a period of at least 70 years. Rulers of the outlying atolls resisted the change, but by the early thirteenth century the new religion had taken root and the succession of 84 sultans in six dynasties had begun.

Two rough and ready fishermen's hangouts with very cheap Maldivian snacks and endless cups of tea.

Shopping
Duty Free Paradise, Umar Shopping Arcade, Chandani Magu. Tel. 32-3864.

Taxis
Dialcab, tel. 32-3132.
New Taxi Service, tel. 32-5757 (24-hours).
Lunghi Taxi Service, tel. 32-5414.
Comfort Taxi Fare, tel. 32-5120, (24-hours).
Regular Taxi Service Co, tel. 32-2454.

Medical Services

Malé's Central Hospital has 84 beds and is on the corner of Sosun Magu and Majeedhee Magu. Tel. 32-2400. It has been run by British aid for the last five years.

Dispensaries can be found on Sosun Magu and on Majeedee Magu, opposite the football stadium.

Dr F Yeganegi, Central Hospital, Malé (Obs & Gyn), Magu Green Life, Handuvaree Higun, Malé 20-21. Tel. 32-2593 (clinic), 32-4293 (home).

Flying Swiss Ambulance Service, Huvadhoo, Marine Drive, Malé 20-06. Tel. 32-4500 (emergency number, 24 hours), 4508-9 (office); tlx 77089 FSA MR. The only mobile medical and

evacuation service in the Maldives. The clinic in Malé has Swiss, German, and Austrian doctors who speak German, English, French, and Italian. A mobile clinic also travels around the atolls. FSA averages about 200 patients a year, many of whom are tourists airlifted from outer islands in emergencies. Most tourist ailments are sustained while scuba diving, usually involving decompression sickness or coral cuts rather than dramatic events like shark bites. FSA has an amphibious boat and a light aircraft. Charges are $200-300 before you're transported off your island, considerably move for a visit or delivery using the boat. The aircraft costs $15 per minute for the flight plus $60 landing charges. No night flights are allowed. Evacuees are usually transferred to Singapore, Colombo, or to an Indian hospital for treatment. The FSA Clinic in Malé charges $45 for a first visit, including simple diagnosis and treatment; overnight bed charges range from $100-1,000. However, we recommend taking out the tourist membership for one month which costs $25 and covers all medical treatment and evacuation from anywhere in the archipelago. Costs for the decompression chamber run to $1,000 per hour, so scuba divers should consider coverage provided by special diving insurance.

Airline Offices

Air Lanka
17 Marine Drive. Tel. 32-3459.
Daily flights to Colombo.

Indian Airlines
Sifaa, Marine Drive. Tel. 32-3003.
Three flights weekly to Trivandrum.

Singapore Airlines
Sisal Corner, 3/5 Faamudheyri Maguy.
Tel. 32-4252. Six flights weekly.

Air Maldives
Marine Drive. Tel. 32-2436.

Emirates
Marine Drive. Tel. 32-5491.
Three flights weekly to Dubai.

Pakistan International Airways
Luxwood #1 Marine Drive. Tel. 32-
3532. Twice weekly to Karachi.

Airline Representatives

LTU/LTS
Faihu Agency, Maaleythila.
Tel. 32-3202.

Austrian Airlines/Condor
Universal Travel Dept, 18 Marine
Drive. Tel. 32-3116.

Royal Nepalese Airlines
Speed Travels, Fareedhee Magu.
Tel. 32-3069.

Lauda Air; Fantasy Trade & Travels
Ltd, Fareedhee Magu. Tel. 32-4668.

Sterling Airways/Balair/Monarch
Voyages Maldives Pvt Ltd,
2 Fareedhee Magu. Tel. 32-2019.

Government Ministries

Ministry of Tourism
2/Fl Ghaazee Bldg, Ameer Ahmed
Magu. Tel. 32-3224, 3596; fax 32-
2512; tlx. 66019 TOURISM MF.

Ministry of Atolls Administration
Faashanaa Bldg, Marine Drive.
Tel. 32-2826, 3070.

**Department of Immigration &
Emigration**
2/Fl Huravee Bldg, Ameeru Ahmed
Magu. Tel. 32-3913.

Ministry of Information
3/Fl Huravee Bldg, Ameeru Ahmed
Magu. Tel. 32-3837.

Banks

Central Bank of the Maldives
Majeedhee Bldg, Marine Drive.
Tel. 32-2291.

Bank of Credit & Commerce
Chandhani Magu. Tel. 32-3605.

Bank of Maldives
Marine Drive. Tel. 32-3095.

Habib Bank Ltd
23 Chandhani Magu. Tel. 32-2051.

State Bank of India
H. Zonaria, Marine Drive.
Tel. 32-3053.

Bank of Ceylon
Alia Bldg, Orchid Magu. Tel. 32-3046.

High Commissions and Embassies

Indian High Commision
Orchid Magu. Tel. 32-3015.

Pakistan Embasssy
Noomaraage, Lily Magu.
Tel. 32-3005.

Sri Lankan High Commission
Orchid Magu. Tel. 32-2845.

Honorary Consuls

France
Mohamed Ismail Manik, 1/27
Chandhani Magu. Tel. 32-3760.

Denmark
Abdulla Saeed, Cyprea, 25 Marine
Drive. Tel. 32-2451.

USA
Rasheeda Mohamed Didi
Mandhuedhuruge, Violet Magu.
Tel. 32-2581.

No other countries have diplomatic
or consular representatives in the
Maldives.

Tour and Resort Operators

The following companies organize a wide range of tours, boat trips, diving
safaris, cruises on yacht *dhonis*, and inter-island boat and speedboat transfers.
Some also operate resorts and hotels they can certainly quote and arrange stays
at resorts. The major companies are ZSS and Voyages Maldives, but the smaller
companies also have suitable cruising boats of different sizes for hire.

ZSS
5 Fiyaathoshi Goalhi, Henveiru.
Tel. 32-2505, 3505; fax 32-4744;
tlx. 66020 ZSS MF.

Phoenix Travel Pvt Ltd
Fasmeeru Hulhagubai. Tel. 32-3587;
tlx. 77080 PHOENIX MF.

Deens Orchid Agency
2/11H. Marine Drive. Tel. 32-2844,
8006, 7450; fax 32-3779.

Voyage Maldives
Fareedhee Magu. Tel. 32-2019, 3017;
fax 32-5336; tlx. 66063 VOYAGE
MF.

Galena Maldives (Pte) Ltd
Orchid Magu. Tel. 32-4742-3.

Altaf Enterprises Ltd, 8 Majeedi
Bazaar. Tel. 32-2890, 3378;
tlx. 66047 ALTAF MF.

Cyprea Ltd, 25 Marine Drive.
Tel. 32-2451; fax. 32-3523.

Safari Tours
Chandhani Magu. Tel. 32-3524;
tlx. 66030 SAFARI MF.

Universal Enterprises
38 Orchid Magu. Tel. 32-2971, 3080;
tlx. 66024 UNIENT MF.

Discovery Tours (Pvt) Ltd
13 Orchid Magu. Tel. 32-3975.

Golden Jet Trade & Travels Ltd
13 Chandhani Magu. Tel. 32-2338;
tlx. 77095 ARIMALÉ MF.

Dolphin Enterprises Ltd
G.Makhumaage. Tel. 32-4445;
tlx. 66081 DOLPHIN MF.

Treasure Island Enterprises
8 Marine Drive. Tel. 32-2537;
tlx. FURANA MF.

Sunland Travel (Pvt) Ltd
2 Kandhili Goalhi. Tel. 32-5543;
tlx. 77064 SUNLAND MF.

Kaimoo Travels
Roanunge. Tel. 32-2212; tlx. 66035
KAIMOO MF.

Olympia
1/Fl Ahmadhee Bazaar. Tel. 32-2037,
3021; tlx. 66094 OLMPIA MF.

Dhirham Travels & Chandling
Faamudheyri Magu. Tel. 32-3369;
tlx. 77050 VALTUR MF

AAA & Trading Co
Chandhani Magu. Tel. 32-4487.

Sea Coast,
Marine Drive. Tel. 32-3364;
tlx. 66021 VCZ MALÉ MF.

Akiri
Marine Drive. Tel. 32-2719;
tlx. 77074 MAKANA MF.

Speed Travels
Faridi Magu. Tel. 32-4280.

Fantasy Trade & Travels
3/2 Fareedhee Magu. Tel. 32-4668;
tlx. 66078 Fantasy MF

Detours
Fasmeeru, H Marine Drive. Tel. 32-5498, 3181, 3587; fax. 32-5499.

Remses Travel Service
Henveiru, Malé. Tel. 32-2854-5;
tlx. 77024 REMSIS MF

Jetan Travels
Marine Drive. Tel. 32-4628.

IMADS Agency
Chandhani Magu. Tel. 32-3441.

Eurasia Agencies,
Meduziyaaraiy Magu. Tel. 32-4538

Akir
Marine Drive. Tel. 32-2719, 2592; fax.
32-3463; tlx. 77065 HOLIDAY MF.

Quest Enterprises
Marine Drive. Tel. 32-3014.

Nazaki Services
Tel. 32-4314-5.

Suntour Maldives
4 Marine Drive. Tel. 32-3467; fax 32-32-3466; tlx. 77065 HOLIDAY MF.

Beach Travel & Tours
1/10 Ameer Ahmed magu.
Tel. 32-4572.

Express
Tel. 32-2432.

Maldivian Traders & Contracting
Tel. 32-2828, 2807-8. Two hovercraft
and eight launches.

Air Transport

Hummingbird Helicopters Pvt. Ltd, Luxwood #2, Marine Drive. Tel. 32-5708; fax. 32-3161. This British company runs a fleet of Sikorskys with picture windows to helipads in Ari and South Malé Atolls.

Atoll	Landing Site	Resort
Ari	Rasdhu	Kuramathi
		Veligandu
Ari	Kandolodhu	Hallaveli
		Maayafushi
		Bathala
		Fesdu
		Ellaido
Ari	Bodufoludhu	Nika Hotel
		Gangehi
		Madoogali
		Velidhu
Ari	Ari Beach	Ari Beach
		Angaga
		Mirihi
		Kudara

Festivals and Holidays

Friday is the national day of prayer and rest; no public practice of religion other than Islam.

State holidays are as follows:

January 1	New Year's Day
July 26	Independence Day, from the British in 1965
November 11	Republic Day, foundation in 1968
November 3	Victory Day, over the Sri Lankan rebels in 1988

Other Celebrations:

National Day	On the first day of Rabee-ul-Awal, victory over the Portuguese in 1578.
Martyr's Day	Death of Sultan Ali VI at the hands of Portuguese in 1558
Huravee Day	Defeat of the Malabaris in 1752
February	Opening of the *majlis* (parliament)

The Great Parade

*I*landed in Male on a Monday, and on the Friday following I went to
see the Sultan's procession returning from the Jama Masjid after
prayers. Friday among Moslems is observed in the same manner as
Sunday with Christians and the first portion of the day is reserved for
prayer.

I left the house about one o'clock as I was told that prayers would
finish about half-past one. The streets seemed quite deserted and
silent and every shop and little boutique was closed.

The whole atmosphere reminded me of nothing so much as a small
township or village in the the north of Scotland on a Sunday. This
effect was further heightened by the fact that it was a dull grey day
with heavy rain clouds working up from the south-west.

I posted myself at a corner near the high walled palace of the
Sultan which commanded a good view of the approach to the mosque.
After a time two men with reddish check turbans, bare to the waist
and wearing dark brown sarongs with two broad stripes at the foot
and edged with white strolled past. These I was told were the nucleus
of the band and some had gone to fetch the drums. Later a figure all
in white wearing a long flowing Arab jibbah and white turban
walked past in a stately manner. This was the Khatib or High Priest
himself who had just finished prayers. Except for the turban he might
have been the photographic negative of a Scotch Minister leaving the
kirk without doffing his black Geneva gown. The Mullah even wore
what appeared very like a round starched collar which closely
resembled the regulation ecclesiastical "dog collar". He was followed
by another white-robed figure carrying a parcel wrapped in a dark
silk cloth which contained the Koran Sharif and other devotional
books. Then appeared some men in white coats or blouses edged with
black, with black shoulder straps and black piping on the sleeves. On
the head was a small red cap attached to a light chain. These were
members of the Police Force or Civil Guard.

Shortly after, about forty of the Sultan's lashkar *or Guards lined up on either side of the road, the leader or colour-sergeant bearing a white furled flag. They all wore check turbans, were bare to the waist and wore the same kind of sarong as the bandsmen, only the colour was dark blue instead of brown. Half of them were armed with lances and the remainder with what looked like very ancient muzzle loaders.*

In the waist cloth of each could be seen the ivory handle, in some cases mounted in silver work, of a dagger much resembling an Arab jambir, *or Persian* khanjar. *The sheaths had ornamental silk tassels at the tip. There was a fanfare of trumpets which heralded the trumpeters with long brass instruments. They were immediately followed by two men with what are known on the Indian frontier as a* saranai—*a kind of clarinet. The moment the trumpets ceased the clarinets burst forth in a weird minor strain. They were accompanied by three drummers, each bearing what is called in India a* dhol *or large drum and a* beru *by the Maldivians. This is beaten with both hands.*

Then came a young man, the nephew of the Sultan, who represented him. Close behind and on either side of him were two umbrella bearers. One of the umbrellas was the white State one used only by the Sultan or his representative, whilst the other was of a delicate rose colour. Both had gilded tops and were elaborately frilled.

The young man wore over a jibbah *of dark green a* saduriya *or waistcoat of salmon colour and had a tarbush on his head. He looked neither to his right nor his left but straight ahead and passed through the gateway leading to the palace.*

The Sultan does not himself always attend Friday prayers, and on this occasion neither the Prince nor the Prime Minister were present as both were indisposed.

The last I saw of the procession as it disappeared through the gate was the umbrellas being twirled around rapidly over the representative's head.

T W Hockly, The Two Thousand Isles, 1935

Religious festivals

May–June   Ramadan
Muslim New Year   First day of Shavval, first month of the Muslim calendar
Eid-ul-Fitr/Kuda Id New moon after Ramadan, feast with sweets and relaxation
Eid al Azha   Two months and ten days later
December–January   Birthday of the Prophet Muhammad

Other Information

National Library
59 Majeedi Magu. Open 9 am–noon and 2 pm–5 pm except Ramadan and Fridays. Tel. 32-3943-5. Opens 9 am–Noon, 2 pm–5 pm.

National Museum
Open 9.30–noon, 3 pm–6 pm except Friday.

DHL
C/o Cyprea Ltd, 25 Marine Drive. Tel. 32-2451; fax. 32-3523.

Skypak
Deens Orchid Agency, Marine Drive. Tel. 32-3779; fax. 32-3877; tlx. 77061 ORCHID MF.

American Express
C/o Universal Enterprises
8 Marine Drive. Tel. 32-3116, 3166; fax. 32-2695.

Novelty Bookshop
Fareedhee Magu. Tel. 32-2564.

Maldivian Game Fish Association
Norber van Stokkum, Kanifinolhu. Tel. 34-3152; fax. 34-4859.

Exceptional Resorts
North Malé Atoll
Kurumba

If you asked an hotel architect to design a resort hotel in paradise this is exactly what he or she might have created: a top-class establishment that still seems just like an international hotel transported to an otherwise deserted island, right down to the drinks in each room's minibar. If staying in a place like this is a novelty for you, that's fine; if you travel on business a lot maybe you'll feel the need to look for something different in the Maldives.

Kurumba is just three kilometres (1.9 miles) from the airport, or ten minutes by speedboat. This was the very first resort to open back in 1972. US$15 million has been spent since then renovating its plush cabana-style architecture and extensive facilities. The one kilometre (half-mile)-long island is attractively landscaped; clumps of bougainvillea, frangipani shrubs, and palm trees ensure privacy between individual cottage units. All 156 twin rooms and eight double-storeyed suites are airconditioned, furnished with imported materials from Singapore, and with fresh flowers daily on the dressing tables. Lots of natural wood and Maldivian-style pillars to create a very natural effect, countered by wall-to-wall carpeting and piped-in music. Connecting rooms and duplexes are available for families.

Facilities are on a grand scale after a massive upgrade in 1987. The reception area has a large polished tile floor, fax and telex are available, as well as IDD telephone in every room. Adjacent large, A-frame buildings house a restaurant, shopping complex, and the Maldives' only conference centre with capacity for 500. Outside is a large freshwater swimming pool—a rarity in the Maldives. The two main restaurants serve Chinese and north Indian food; a 24-hour coffee shop completes the hotel atmosphere. The food selection is suitably broad, accented on fresh seafood. The *all' aperto* dining area on the sand turns into a seafood barbecue at night. Attention to detail is high, right down to the clean table linen, hovering staff, and freshly cut imported orchids. Food is flown in thrice weekly from Japan and New Zealand, and is correspondingly highly priced. The bar, nestling under a huge *dhoni*-shaped A-frame and outfitted with nautical furnishings, is one of the best stocked in the archipelago. Close to Malé, Kurumba attracts day-and-evening trippers, and offers live entertainment in its strobe-lit open-air nightly disco.

There is a large fleet of speedboats for pleasure trips, glass-bottomed boats to tour the reef, day or night-fishing for garoupa and red snapper, plus the range of sailing, windsurfing, and scuba facilities. The large diving school run by EuroDivers of Switzerland is well rated by the expatriate community in Malé. Uniquely, Kurumba possesses an excellent sports gym complete with jacuzzi, three floodlit tennis courts, a second smaller freshwater swimming pool, and an airconditioned billiards room manned by a bow tied attendant.

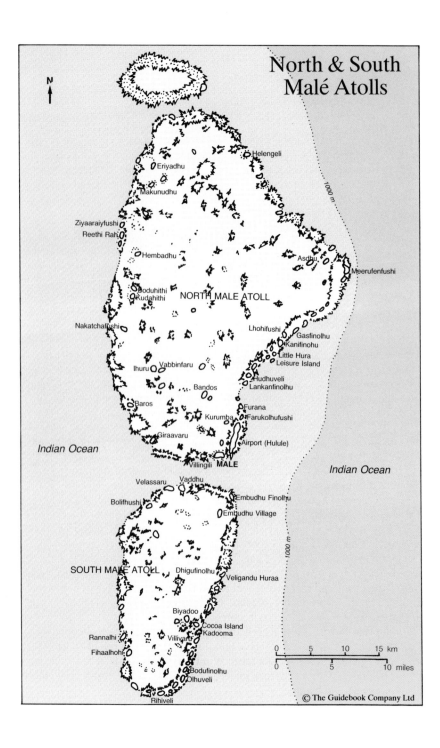

North & South
Malé Atolls

N

Helengeli
Eriyadhu
Makunudhu
Ziyaaraiyfushi
Reethi Rah
Hembadhu
Asdhu
Meerufenfushi
Boduhithi
Kudahithi
NORTH MALE ATOLL
Nakatchafushi
Lhohifushi
Gasfinolhu
Kanifinohu
Little Hura
Leisure Island
Ihuru
Vabbinfaru
Hudhuveli
Lankanfinolhu
Bandos
Baros
Furana
Kurumba
Farukolhufushi
Giraavaru
Airport (Hulule)
Villingili
MALE

Indian Ocean

Indian Ocean

Velassaru
Vaddhu
Bolifhushi
Embudhu Finolhu
Embudhu Village

SOUTH MALE ATOLL
Dhigufinolhu
Veligandu Huraa

Biyadoo
Cocoa Island
Rannalhi
Villivaru
Kadooma
Fihaalhohi
Bodufinolhu
Olhuveli
Rihiveli

1000 m

1000 m

| 0 | | 5 | | 10 | | 15 km |

| 0 | | 5 | | 10 miles |

© The Guidebook Company Ltd

Summary
Near the airport with excellent facilities, but expensive.
Price: Double-storied suites $350 daily; other rooms are $160.
Transfer: A fifteen-minute *dhoni*-ride from Malé or the airport, for $10.
Booking: Tel. 34-3081/4, 34-2324; fax. 34-3885; tlx.77083 Kurumba MF.
Or through local agent Universal Enterprises, 38 Orchid Magu,
Malé: Tel. 32-3080/2971/3512; fax. 32-2678; tlx. 66024
UNIENT MF.

Reethi Rah

This Swiss-run resort of 100 beds is one of the loveliest in the archipelago, secluded and chic, fully living up to its local name of Medhufinolhu, 'the beautiful island', and belying its ten-year age. In truth, like most of the small islands, it's little more than a sandbank capped with vegetation and can be strolled around in a leisurely 15 minutes. The setting is simply superb, with a protective reef on the leeward side enclosing a broad, shallow lagoon of glass-smooth translucent water, perfect for learning to dive or windsurf. The 50 palm-thatched, whitewashed coral bunglows blend harmoniously with the lush vegetation and well-raked white sand, and are strung along the eastern beach facing the sea linked by a single path. At night the only sound is the whisper of the sea.

Interiors of the individual units are simple, meticulously clean, and aesthetically pleasing with plenty of natural wood and coir matting. Ventilation is provided by an ingenious woven screen that leaves the room partially open to the sky, a nice Maldivian touch. Standard amenities include a bathroom with shower using desalinated hot and cold water. Reethi Rah attracts mainly Swiss and German executive types who return year after year. It discourages package tours to protect its intimacy. The accomplished Swiss chef ensures high standards to European tastes, and daily menus with plenty of seafood, including lobster, and tropical fruits. The kitchen can fulfill most breakfast requests, from pancakes to delicious fluffy omelettes, and serves an excellent espresso. Lavish buffets of Maldivian food, mainly curries and grilled fish, complement continental menus. The main restauarant has a billowy canvas roof with prettily laid-out tables on a floor of soft sand next to the well-stocked bar. Tucked away elsewhere on the island another hideaway bar hovers over the water on stilts with stunning views. A good place to watch the migratory cranes and terns. The bar has a well-stocked cellar of imported French wines, champagnes, and German beers. The latter is all drawn from casks as cans despoil the environment.

Both the EuroDivers scuba school and the Maldives' base of the renowned Swiss Mistral windsurfing school have brand-new equipment and offer daily lessons for beginners at reasonable rates. Windsurfing use starts at $165 for ten hours for beginners Other activities include catamaran sailing, snorkelling, table tennis, volleyball, and badminton.

Summary:
A delightful haven of peace in pristine surroundings, run with Swiss excellence.
Price: Peak season, full board, s/d $81/126; low season, s/d $57/94.
Transfer: Two-and-a-half hours by wooden launch, $46.
Booking: Tel. 34-2077; tlx. 77046 RERARE MF.

Vabbinfaru

This is an exceptionally beautiful island—a personal favourite. It was one of
the original five resorts which launched the Maldives as a tourist destination in
the early 1970s, a headstart enhanced by some excellent construction work by
the French owner and his father. It is still privately managed by a French couple
who have been there for six years. The resort, staffed by ten Europeans and forty
Maldivians, is very popular with Swiss and Belgians. The emphasis is suitably
gastronomic; the French chef even makes fresh croissants, pastries and bread
in the island's bakery. Decadent patisseries and pancakes laced with Grand
Marnier and chocolate, creme caramels, succulent brioches, are all par for the
course. The main restaurant has a tall roof and is open to the elements atrium-
style so that sun, sand and sea blend together. The set menus for lunch and
dinner are excellent.

Vabbinfaru is quite small with only 30 bungalows set back from lovely sandy
avenues of coconut palms, 'magoo' and bougienvillea shrubs. Two bungalows
lie near the sea, the waves lapping at the front door on a tiny private beach; these
are for families, the split-level rooms housing three or four beds. The other
cottages are thatched, circular, airy A-frames built using natural screw pine
matting, *satta* mats and *kunnar* rattan—a simple decor with a pleasant and
natural feel emphasized by the whitewashed coral walls and the spacious tiled
bathrooms. The resort shop is well-stocked with fashionable clothes made by
Barbara Sansoni, a Sri Lankan designer, with lovely jewellery and scarves.
Very elegant and continental, it's by far the nicest shop in the Maldives.
The aviary adds to the air of refinement.

The beach is perfect for swimming and snorkelling, a gentle smooth lagoon
with a fine sand bottom is protected by the house reef about 50 metres (165 feet)
out. There is a fully equipped diving school. Other activities range from catamaran sailing to fishing, windsurfing, and mini tennis. A speedboat is available
for hire.

Summary
Very chic and Gallic.
Price: Peak season, full board, s/d $120/200; low season 40
                   percent less.
Transfer: Half an hour by speedboat.
Booking: Tel. 34-3147; fax. 34-3843; tlx. 77026 VABBIN MF.

South Malé Atoll
Rihiveli

I'll never forget arriving at this resort, the boat cutting through aquamarine waters and heralded by a school of dolphins. Opened in 1983, it certainly belongs in the 'very special' category. Frenchman Pitt Pietersonne lives here year-round with his family and runs the 89-bed resort in a very personalized, idiosyncratic style with 12 French staff and 70 locals. Rihiveli, meaning 'silver sands', attracts mainly French visitors with smaller numbers of discerning Australians, Italians, Germans and British. One of its manager's quirks: groups (as opposed to individuals) of Japanese or Germans are not encouraged as a rule, the autocratic Pietersonne insisting that it is impossible to create harmony among such disparate guests, especially over the sensitive subject of what appears on the dinner table!

There are 36 cottages, each very spacious with aesthetic natural-fibre furnishings, in beautifully landscaped seclusion. Named rather than numbered, they are widely scattered over the island to ensure privacy. Each has its own hammock nearby, a nice languid touch. The water supplied in the rooms is a mix of collected rainwater, well water and desalinated water. The restaurant is built over the sea with a *dhoni*-style servery. The view is remarkable and the food marvellous, mainly French and Italian dishes, with plenty of fresh fish, fruit and salads and Maldivian buffets once a week. A good selection of wine and beer is stocked. The day I arrived the set lunch consisted of smoked fish in a delicious coconut sauce, followed by a salad Niçoise served with fresh fruit juices— refreshing and simply superb. Not suprisingly, Rihiveli attracts a high rate of repeat visitors, people convinced they have located their vision of paradise. Those who return four times are awarded their own wooden chair etched with their name beneath the leafy trees in the open-air, sand-swirled bar, guarded by a trio of parrots. Rhivelhi tries to do just a little bit more than other resorts. Local dance and drum music figures in the weekly island programme and you can take tea and coconut flesh with the Maldivian staff every evening in the staff restaurant.

Rihiveli also scores highly for its amenities and activities. Free windsurfing, snorkelling, day and night fishing, volleyball, and tennis are offered year-round. Yoga and aerobics classes are held every evening in the open-air gymnasium. You can hire a catamaran, or go water-skiing and parasailing at a reasonable rate. You can also go trawling for deep-sea fish, or fish the local way with a hand line; the boat hire rate is $16 per hour. The boutique stocks high-fashion beachwear, costume jewellery, books, videos, and souvenirs. You can rent underwater video cameras and equipment, have slide film developed, or get someone to take photos or a video of your holiday.

Diving enthusiasts rate Rihiveli's Eurodivers school highly for the emphasis placed on personalized tuition where classes are never for more than six people.

All four instructors have spent lots of time in the Maldives and are very experienced; PADI courses are offered for both beginners and advanced divers, and both day and night trips can be arranged. Richard Walker, the tanned Brit who runs the school, prefers that guests take their time to learn and is critical of other resorts' 'diving factory' attitude. He recommends that a beginner should spend at least nine rather than five days on the basic course and that two dives a day is enough. The Scuba-Pro equipment is top-class.

A converted *dhoni*, the *Shadas*, is moored here. It can be booked for simple day excursions or longer safari cruises at $480 per day for six people

inclusive. A free three-day cruise on *Shadas* around South Malé Atoll can be applied for during the low season between 1 April and 30 October. Excursions and barbecues can be arranged on three tiny deserted islands close to Rihveli, easily reached by wading through the powder-soft sandy lagoon. You can also hire motorized *dhonis* and speedboats. Excursions from Rihiveli include trips to local fishing villages, other tourist islands, and a full-day picnic off-island. Guradoo, a local fishing village with a population of 800, is 45 minutes away by *dhoni*. Felidhu, the island of birds, is about two hours away.

Summary
Aesthetic environment, with careful attention to detail and the personal touch, though the manager's autocratic style is not to every taste.

Price: Peak season s/d about $160/180; low season 25 percent less.
Transfer: 40 kilometres (25 miles) from the airport.
Booking: Tel. 34-3731; fax. 34-4775; tlx. 66072 PITTMAT MF.

Vaadhu

It's easy to see why this small and lush resort appeals to its predominantly Japanese clientele. Here you can lie in a steaming black marble bath, eat room service sushi, clinch a business deal on the Telephone to Osaka, and gaze out across the wide blue ocean. Designed by a Japanese, managed by a Japanese, and with a staff that includes a sushi chef and Japanese diving instructor, it also has Japanese-style prices.

There are three styles of accommodation in this 80-bed resort, each quite different. Top of the line are seven thatched 'Floating Cottages', impressively luxurious structures built on stilts over the lagoon and connected by wooden walkways. Inside, a glass table gives you the impression of being in your own aquarium. At night the blue of the sea is lit by soft lights and tropical fish appear to swim around on your floor. High tech facilities include an IDD telephone in every room, even the bathroom. Two suites sleeping four, in two bedrooms, are particularly gorgeous; the other five cottages sleep two, in twin beds. All are airconditioned with sake-stocked refrigerators, colour-coordinated plush interiors, furnishings, and wool carpet— a clever and tasteful blend of natural woods and fibres with modern comforts. Even the curtains are remote-controlled. The bathrooms are accented with black marble and Maldivian *satta* weave screens. Every cottage has a private balcony.

The other 24 rooms are grouped in a small airconditioned block called the 'Sunrise Wing', much cheaper but not half as nice. The main difference is that they are not as private, romantic or delightful as the stilt cottages, despite their freshwater showers. All rooms offer the chance to take all meals by room service if you choose, a service popular with Japanese newly weds.

There are two relaxed open-air beach bars with sand underfoot. One on stilts is particularly attractive, a construction of bamboo and natural thatch adorned with huge dangling chandeliers made of shells. The night I stayed at Vaadhu a crane was nesting on the roof and made a beautiful sight against the setting sun. The food is excellent, with a set menu which is either continental, Japanese, Chinese or French-Italian, plus a weekly Maldivian buffet. The Japanese specialities include sushi, miso soup, and excellent tuna sashimi.

Vaddhu's location just off the channel separating North and South Malé atolls, offers a rich variety of marine life. Nearby waters boasts dolphins; sharks of various kinds including whale sharks; eagle and manta rays; and thousands of spectacular coral reef fish. It has its own diving centre with instructors offering training for both NAUI and PADI courses. The diving resort course of three lessons costs $140; the PADI Open Water course $320; PADI Advanced Open Water Course $170. A dive with full equipment costs $30; six days with basic equipment is $210, and with full equipment, $240. Other activities include excursions in a glass-bottomed boat, day and night fishing, use of a catamaran, water-skiing and scootering, and snorkelling. And there are even plans to introduce a performing dolphin to the surrounding waters, to greet new arrivals.

Summary
A stylish but expensive mixture of Japanese lifestyle and high technology; the best sushi in the Maldives; 14 of the best diving spots nearby; almost exclusively Japanese clientele

Price: Peak season—full board per week, standard room $120–160; water cottage $220–360; cottage suite $395–670. Low season—full board per week, standard room $80–100; water cottage $195–300; cottage suite $325–560.

Transfer: 15 minutes by speedboat, $15 return.

Booking: Tel. 34-3397; fax. 34-3977; tlx. 77016 VADOO MF; Cable–Paradise.

Cocoa Island

My first impression of the tiny island of Makunufushi from the deck of a *dhoni* was of a graceful, barefooted figure walking towards me clad in designer hessian. Cocoa is a dream island run like a private club, a 16-bed exclusive bolt hole for those for whom luxurious seclusion is as important as the glorious suntan, the unlimited water sports, glassy smooth sea, and pristine natural beauty to be found elsewhere in the Maldives.

Tucked in amidst the bougainvillea and linked by sandy pathways, the island's eight A-frame cottages are havens of primitive aestheticism with a very

Mediterranean or Polynesian feel. All the buildings rely on indigenous materials—rough, whitewashed, textured coral walls, palm wood beams, palm leaf thatch, and lacquered *satta* ceilings—and blend harmoniously with their surroundings. Inside, the 'floor' is smooth sand which feels like silk to walk on, another unusual and inspired touch. Wooden stairs lead up to a loft where the bed is draped with a large mosquito net. Each of the cottages is designed to accommodate two or three persons and sits right on the beach. Despite the deliberate omission of airconditioning, the rooms remain cool inside. All bathroom units are equipped with shower, toilet, and 220V electrical outlets.

The impressively stocked bar sits on stilts above the lagoon, and is connected to the beach by a boardwalk. The restaurant produces high-quality meals for a small number of people, with the emphasis on fish specialities.

Cocoa's great advantage is its water sports facilities. The shallow, sheltered lagoon with its sandy bottom offers ideal conditions for sailing, windsurfing, and water-skiing. A nearby sandbank almost a kilometre (half a mile) long is perfect for those wishing to bathe or tan in seclusion. On the north side of the island, 30 metres (66 feet) from the water's edge, is a coral reef which drops off into the depths of the ocean, perfect for snorkelling.

Summary
One of the most beautiful havens in the Maldives, but can be difficult to book. The management led by ex-*Playboy* photographer, Eric Klemm, does not encourage casual visitors to linger.

Price: Peak season $250, slight reduction for low season.

Transfer: 40 kilometres (25 miles) from the airport, two hours by *dhoni* or 45 minutes by speedboat.

Booking: Tel. 960-34-3713; tlx. 77037 Cocoa MF.

Ari Atoll
Nika
Nika is the designer fantasy of an Italian architect-turned-vagabond, Giovanni Borgo, who leased the island and built his first bungalow to live like a tropical prince in the early 1980s. He later added several more to turn his Robinson Crusoe island into a quiet hotel. The resort is named after the rare banyan *nika* tree that stands in the the middle of the island.

More than 300 tons of soil have been imported from Sri Lanka, and the island is the best vegetated in the archipelago, especially noted for its large trees. Papayas, mangosteens, mangoes, watermelons, salad vegetables, and bananas, are all grown here—and ten gardeners are employed just to pick up all the leaves.

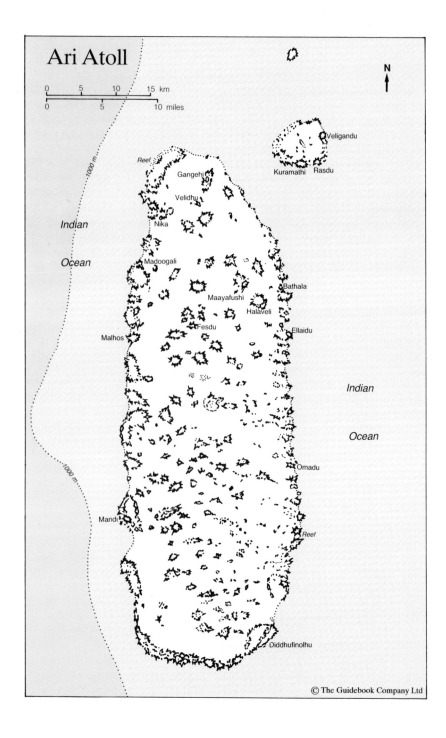

Under the command of Matteo Bellassi from Milan, Nika attracts all sorts of people and a range of nationalities, mainly Italians, Germans, Japanese, British, and French. Nika sets its clocks two hours ahead of Malé, a common trick in the Maldives so that guests can feel utterly relaxed about leaving in time to catch their plane. Guests are given a plastic watch set to 'Nika Time'when they arrive, which they can keep as a memento.

There are 25 bungalows, upgraded in 1987, and each is shaped to resemble a giant shell and built in a mixture of coral and whitewashed cement. Breadfruit leaf-imprints decorate the walls, the high ceilings are thatched and decorated with tortoiseshell, and the slatted wooden windows let in gentle breezes. Each bungalow has a small private beach and garden, large mosquito net, IDD telephone, and freshwater showers with hot water. The nicest bungalow suite is the Sultans' Bungalow with its old Sri Lankan furniture; the two bedrooms are ideal for a family. The 80-odd staff speak several European languages. The restaurant is tastefully decorated with *lunghi*-style tablecloths and huge cowrie shells. The buffet-style food is excellent: fresh pasta, delicious cakes, and fresh fruit from the resort's own trees. There is a fine range of Italian wines and French champagnes.

Nika is blessed with some superb diving spots, including the world-famous Fish-head Reef just two and a half hours' away by boat, where you can expect to see eagles and sting rays and huge mantas, especially in February. There are also some nonaggressive white-tipped reef sharks. The German instructor never lets classes exceed eight people, PADI progression courses up to Professional level are available. There's also a huge open-air aquarium which makes for fascinating viewing. It contains many nurse sharks, large turtles, stingrays, and many brightly coloured tropical fish that are fed every day on scraps from the resort's tables. Your children will find it hard to keep away.

You can make excursions to the deserted island of Viamafaru, to Kuda Finolhu (literally, 'very small island'), and to Bodu Folhudhu, a nearby fishing village. Nika also has a jetty where yachts can moor overnight and a nice natural grass tennis court.

Summary

Great diving opportunities; relaxed atmosphere, but not as informal as some other small resorts.

Price: Peak season $170-340 per week; low season $75-150.

Transfer: 67 kilometres (42 miles) from Malé. Hummingbird helicopters connects nearby Bodu Folhudhu with Singapore Airlines' weekly flight, followed by a 25-minute boat transfer, price $250; speedboat transfer from Malé takes about two hours, price $200.

Booking: Book one year in advance for peak season; low season is less of a problem. Tel. 34-4616; fax. 34-4777; tlx. 66124 NIKA MF.

Gangehi

Ultra-chic Italian resort designed for Club Vacanze, twinned with Bodohithi and Alimata in Felidhu atoll; very popular with Italian honeymooners. A beautifully landscaped wooden walkway encircles the island and is raised to protect the sand and the carefully maintained undergrowth and shrubbery.The walkway is lit up at night to look like a string of fireflies ringing the island; very beautiful. The lagoon is very large.

Opened in 1987, Gangehi has 25 rooms, eight of which are in the lagoon and whose balconies are perfect places to laze before taking a private swim. The others are set back in the vegetation and surrounded by bougainvillea. All rooms are furnished and decorated to a high standard, with *kunaar*-patterned bedcovers on black wooden beds overlooking a spacious balcony, Thai cane chairs, black-tiled bathrooms with wood fittings, bidet and bathroom scales (a very Italian touch!), lots of mirrors, slats to provide private shade, thatched roofs, and Polynesian-style sliding doors. All rooms are airconditioned, with a well-stocked minibar, telephone, and nice touches like bathrobes and scented toilet paper.

The restaurant and bar are interconnected and look over the sea. The centre-piece of the tall thatched A-frame area is a giant aquarium in which lurks the poisonous Maldivian stonefish, a small shark, and many brilliantly coloured tropical fish. The bar serves Lavazza coffee and the best cappuccino in the Maldives, amid a flurry of beautiful dragonflies. Simplicity is the order of the day, with design continuity, a décor of glazed terracotta pots, and fine tableware. There is also a resident pianist. The food, served in three daily buffets, is uniformly fresh with the emphasis on fruits and juices like papaya and mango, delicious fish, innumerable pasta dishes, and wonderful wines.

Gangehi is normally fully booked from December to May, almost entirely by Italians, though some Germans and French also come. Only in the low season, during the European summer, is it relatively easy for individual tourists to book. The two diving instructors don't offer diving courses, though the 12-year old twin resort on Alimata does have a diving school. The waters inside the large lagoon, however, are excellent for water sports or zipping about in the fleet of speedboats or canoes. Excursions to the uninhabited Mathiveri Finolhu, which actually belongs to Nika, can be arranged; honeymoon couples can be 'marooned' there for several hours in idyllic isolation.

Summary

Beautiful, sophisticated, but definitely for the well heeled. Almost exclusively Italian clientele.

Price: Singles or doubles $130 per night in the high season.
Transfer: 70 kilometres (44 miles) from the airport.
Booking: Tel. & fax. 35-0505.

Choosing a Resort

There are now more than 63 purpose-built tourist resorts in the Maldives, and after a lull in the late 1980s more are coming onstream every year. Tourist development in the archipelago has growth rings as obvious as those of trees. The most established, and often the most popular resorts, are centred around Malé in the North Malé Atoll. A second group spread in the late 1970s throughout South Malé Atoll. The present wave of expansion is taking place in Ari Atoll, where nine or ten were opening during the 1991–92 season. Vaavu Atoll will be next. The authorities are sure they are on the right track keeping tourists basically segregated from the indigenous population and pushing resorts further up-market by making the terms of their leases more stringent. Many resorts are being renovated and upgraded as their leases come up for renewal or as the market changes, most recently because of an influx of Japanese tourists with higher expectations. Resorts that have expanded and upgraded recently include Kurumba, Kanifinolhu, Bandos, Bodhufinolhu, Kuredhdhu, Kuramathi, Vaadhu, and Lhohifushi.

There is little danger that the Maldives will become heavily over exploited as has happened with other tourist destinations like Pattaya in Thailand or parts of Bali in Indonesia. For one thing, the government is concerned to isolate foreigners from the locals, something which a massive, uncontrolled influx would jeopardize. It is keen to keep that 'quality feel' for as long as the country's stretched resources can cope. Secondly, the Maldives can offer the best of one type of holiday: a sea and sun resort-style vacation with the chance to learn a new sport thrown in, in waters that are among the top three diving grounds in the world. It has none of the other cultural attractions (or, in the case of Pattaya, sleazy sexploitation) that travellers associate with Asia. Thus it continues to attract a hard core of water sports enthusiasts and honeymooners rather than singles or families. Many resorts, notably the smaller ones, report high return rates, often year after year.

The country also appeals to the newest generation of travel spenders, the Japanese, who love the combination of pristine beaches, convivial company— often of fellow honeymooners—and laid-on activities in a theme environment. The government says it is planning to take back some of the resort islands to house the ever-growing local population, a move which is becoming more important as overcrowding increases in Malé. However, this is not certain as the tourist dollar is a vital and stable form of income; a few islands that can be absorbed easily may change, but not many more.

As everywhere, though, you get what you pay for and there's sufficient range to make it worth carefully considering your priorities (and your budget.) With the exception of a few very exclusive resorts, most islands are not noted for their solitude or privacy. You will almost certainly be isolated on a tiny island for

your holiday, but in the peak season you are likely to be joined by up to 100 or so other tourists. Many of the best resorts are practically block booked by an agent with a particular style or nationality of clientele, so your choice is often predetermined by those listed in your own country's brochures.

Choose your island with care. Many people go to another island for a second visit to the archipelago only to be disappointed that their second choice wasn't as good as their first. The best of the Maldives costs quite a lot to enjoy, but in most cases it is worth it. Several places, however, claim to be much more than they really are, and have prices to match. Others give the impression of being probably quite dreadful, the advance warning, perhaps, of mass tourism that is so far only mildly evident. A few, notably the Italian and Japanese resorts, caters so carefully for their client that it would be a pleasure for almost anyone to experience them. If you feel like being private, you can do so in the Maldives. You can also learn to windsurf or scuba dive, and are guaranteed a good tan in the space of a fortnight in the right season, when northern latitudes are swathed in winter.

Accomodation is generally in thatched cottages or bungalows—known as 'cabanas'—with an attached bathroom containing a bath and/or shower and a small veranda usually facing the sea and overlooking the beach. It's unusual to find any building higher than a single storey; only a half dozen resorts have even a two-storey building on their islands. You don't have to move very far up-market to find detached accomodation that offers an extra degree of seclusion and comfort. This guide stresses such resorts, but even the spartan places can be appealing as a way to 'get away from it all'.

Practically every resort offers a range of outdoor facilities that includes diving, snorkelling, sailing, water-skiing, parasailing, and catamaran sailing. Other activities, sometimes outdoors, sometimes indoors in special gymnasia (the latest indication of the upwardly mobile resort) include volleyball, badminton, tennis, table tennis and aerobics. Almost all resorts can organize other activities such as day and night-time fishing excursions. On the social side, all the large resorts offer modern attractions like a disco floor, evening videos, cultural shows, island hopping tours, a souvenir shop, and sedentary board games. All of them have a tiny mosque in the compound for the local workers, just to remind you that you aren't in a completely rootless paradise.

Visitors tend to have two main complaints; food and fresh water. The food can be bland and uninspiring in some resorts. This is more true in the larger ones which find it hard to cook for several hundred guests at the same time while relying even partially on local supplies for fresh produce. They all have to import large amounts of recognizably packaged western food to complement what is available locally. Smaller resorts can do much better, and indeed offer some of the best seafood you can find in Asia. I have selected those places where I was particularly struck by the combination of food, appearance, and service. If this is of supreme importance my advice is stay close to the Italians who are the most demanding visitors.

There is a general lack of fresh water for washing, and a common criticism of some resorts' reliance on water tapped from wells beneath the islands, which is inevitably salty. Remember, too, that water rarely cools properly in the tropics. It is difficult to get soap to lather, and shampoo can't do its job well, leaving you with a head of sticky, stiff hair. In the past, almost all the resorts used to pump water from the ground and filter it through the sand. The resulting water is quite unpleasant, even when boiled. To combat this, well over half the resorts now have desalinization plants, something that is now seen as a necessity; others collect fresh rainwater in barrels as a supplement. Some will provide fresh water 24 hours a day, while others restrict it to a few hours in the morning or evening. Occasionally the desalinization system breaks down or there are long periods without rain; then it's back to the bore hole water and sea water. It's probably better not to care too much, but hot water can be sorely missed even on a desert island. Visitors will find, however, that there are always flasks of bottled drinking water in rooms and at meals.

Resorts Versus Cruising

Free and independent travellers are not encouraged to roam around the Maldives. It is not impossible to do so, but it is far from easy and only a certain type of person would feel the need to journey like this in the Maldives compared with, say, Indonesia which would repay such endeavours to a much greater extent. Back in the early 1980s a few hippie travellers made it here, though it was never quite on the trail which paused at Goa en route to Bali. However, in 1985 the government tightened things up and introduced a permit system which made it impossible to stay anywhere that's inhabited outside of Malé, and not a resort, without getting permission first (though paradoxically it still seems you're free to use uninhabited islands as you please). A bed tax was established and all the guesthouses were closed down. Permission, which is granted by the Inter-Atolls Administration, is hard to get without a bona fide reason. One way out is to go by boat and to stay on board; the bed tax is levied anyway, but no one is going to cast you adrift at night.

Have a second look at the special section on organizing a cruise (page 30). This is the only real alternative to a prebooked and packaged resort holiday. Check the list of tour operators (page 85). They can advise on the types of boats available (generally you can stop over at resorts to pick up essential supplies, like drinks, in the evenings). If you like your freedom the feeling of thrusting across the bluest of blue oceans looked after by a skilled and sinewy Maldivian crew is hard to match. Even if you have a language problem they will help you choose an itinerary which the boat can manage in the time available and given the prevailing weather. The European operators listed will provide a more comfortable service in many ways but are mainly busy servicing diving groups willing to pay the extra to get to new dive sites. Study the prices. If there are a group of you it can work out cheaper to stay afloat and it really does provide an unforgettable escape if you are the kind of person who can't stay still on a beach for a week or ten days.

The next big growth area will probably be big-game fishing, as practised in Florida and on the Great Barrier Reef. The Maldives' no-net-trawling rule means that the big surface-fighting fish just get bigger: yellow-finned tuna up to 270 kilos (600 pounds), swordfish and sailfish around 70 kilos (150 pounds), black marlin up to 635 kilos (1,400 pounds). The best time to chase game fish is in the early morning between 5 am and 11 am. Specially equipped boats for up to four fishermen can be hired for around $65 per hour. Contact the Maldivian Big Game Fishing Association.

Finally, think about taking in another country on the way out or back, a diversion that your travel agent can very easily arrange. Sri Lanka is astonishingly beautiful and largely devoid of tourists in recent years; cheap air tickets are also available on the national airline, Air Lanka.

Description of Resorts

The following pages describe all the resorts currently open to tourists in the Maldives. Around half of these, usually the ones with more detailed entries, were visited by the author during the 1989-90 season. Information on the remaining resorts has been culled from a variety of sources. When choosing a resort, look carefully at the brochures issued by travel companies and carefully compare the facilities on offer against those listed here. You can get a pretty good feel for the resorts by the way they describe themselves in this literature as they always want to stress their best points; scrutinize the pictures closely, too.

I have graded resorts into just two categories, as only a small number stand out as truly exceptional. This is not to say that the rest are not wonderful locations for a great holiday, but simply results from the difficulty of grading resorts that are very often different. You will need to consider several criteria when selecting the best resort for your own needs. A standard resort might be just what you're looking for, or simply what you can afford for the type of holiday you want. Whatever your choice, don't forget that the archipelago contains places of outstanding natural beauty, the like of which would be hard to find outside of the remotest of Pacific islands. Look forward to the sight of an endless horizon, radiant waters, and a crisp, clear sky in twenty different shades of blue from sparklingly transparent to the deepest azure. The Maldives manages to combine that beauty with relatively easy access, especially if you are coming from Europe, in a pristine environment perfect for water sports.

Room rates shown here were in effect during the 1989-90 season. Slight increases can be expected, especially in the light of rising petroleum prices which affect transportation and electricity generation costs. All prices quoted are in US dollars per day per room. There is a wide variation between the rates quoted given by the resorts themselves and the prices a travel agent can get for you. Tour operators offer a discount of up to 40 percent on listed prices and everything is discretionary during the off-season, i.e. outside of the November–April high season, with discounts averaging 25 percent. Some resorts halve their rates out of season, others only shave them. Talk to the operators direct, or to a local agent if you want to find out an accurate price. Many are reluctant to reveal their Fixed Individual Tariff, the rate that applies to people that just turn up on the night (not an easy thing to do in the Maldives anyway). Package deals work out much cheaper and are by far the most popular way of arranging a holiday in the Maldives.

The Atolls

The 26 atolls of the Maldives are spread out across several hundred miles and grouped for convenience into 19 administrative groups. They have long names that are hard to pronounce, but the government has helpfully made it easier by listing them alphabetically running from north to south. Most people therefore identify the atoll group from the assigned letter of the Roman alphabet, from A to S. The same system is used for boat registration throughout the archipelago, so if you want to know where a boat is going to, or where it is from, look for the single letter painted on the prow. Since most *dhonis* ply between their own atoll and Malé this is a good way of choosing which *masdhoni* to approach if you want to get a ride. Good luck!

North Thiladhunmathi—A
At the farthest edge of the archipelago and 26 kilometres (160 miles) north of Malé, with around 16 inhabited islands and a population of some 9,000. Its capital is on Diddu. Utheemu was the birthplace of Sultan Mohamed Thakurufaanu, the vanquisher of the Portuguese in 1573; it has a small museum. Kela was a British base during the Second World War, the northern counterpart of Gan. Turukunu is the most northern island of all, and is noted for its pretty girls and dancing.

South Thiladhunmathi—B
The capital is Nolivaranfaru, though the most populous island is Kuluduffushi, most of whose workers have already migrated to Malé, leaving only some 12,000 in the atoll, which is served by one of the Maldives' two regional hospitals. It also boasts the highest island in the archipelago, Faridu, elevation 6 metres (20 feet), and principally famous for its toddy. Lots of wreck dives, especially near Mukunudu, which also has some of the best fishing grounds.

North Miladhunmadulu—C
Just under 200 kilometres (124 miles) from Malé, with 15 inhabited islands and a population of around 7,000. The capital, Faru Kolu Funadu, has a good harbour and the ruins of an ancient mosque and 700-year-old tombstones. The atoll is famed for the turtles that breed on its beaches.

South Miladhunmadulu—D
Numbering 14 inhabited islands among almost 60 that aren't, and with a total population of around 6,500. Velidhu and Holudu are the most populous islands though Munadu is the capital. A 40-foot ruin on Landu appears to be a relic left by Thor Heyerdahl's mysterious ancient traveller, the *Redin*.

North Maalhosmadulu—E
Sixteen peopled islands and 65 uninhabited ones make up this atoll, whose capital is Ungoofaru. A total of 9,000 people live here and Kandoludu even suffers same problem as Malé, overpopulation. It has the best fishing in the whole archipelago, especially near Alifushi, an island famous for its skilled boatmakers and site of the main government boat yard supplying *dhonis*

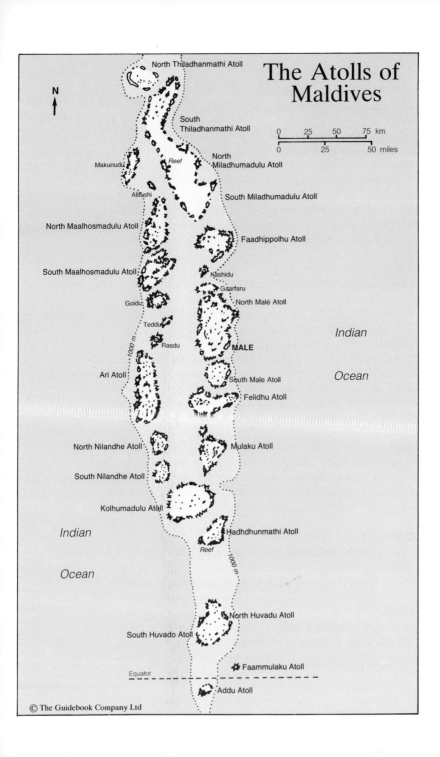

The Atolls of Maldives

North Thiladhanmathi Atoll

South Thiladhanmathi Atoll

Makunudu

Reef

North Miladhumadulu Atoll

Alifushi

South Miladhumadulu Atoll

North Maalhosmadulu Atoll

Faadhippolhu Atoll

South Maalhosmadulu Atoll

Kashidu

Gaarfaru

Goidu

North Malé Atoll

Teddu

Rasdu

MALE

Indian

Ari Atoll

South Male Atoll

Felidhu Atoll

Ocean

North Nilandhe Atoll

Mulaku Atoll

South Nilandhe Atoll

Kolhumadulu Atoll

Hadhdhunmathi Atoll

Indian

Reef

Ocean

North Huvadu Atoll

South Huvado Atoll

Faammulaku Atoll

Equator

Addu Atoll

N

0   25   50   75   km

0   25   50   miles

1000 m

1000 m

© The Guidebook Company Ltd

throughout the country. Renowned craftsmen also live on Inguraidu and Innamaadu.

South Maalhosmadulu—F

Thirteen inhabited islands and more than 50 that are not, with a population of about 7,000. The best fishing grounds are near Eyadafushi, Hitadu, and Tuladu. *Feyli* weaving (for women's sarongs) and lacquerwork boxes are manufactured on Tulusdhu and Fehendu islands. Fuludu was the site of the shipwreck of the *Corbin,* which kept François Pyrard de Laval in the Maldives. It was also the place of banishment of a German tourist who murdered his girlfriend in the mid-70s. Goidu and Fehendu are also prison islands.

Faadhippolhu—G

Just 120 kilometres (75 miles) from Malé, Faadhippolhu comprises four inhabited islands with the capital on Naifaru. The fishing is good, second only to South Maalnosmadulu. Handicrafts include mother-of-pearl and black coral.

Malé—H

Includes North and South Malé Atolls and the smaller Gaafaru; the atoll office is on Thulusdhu. Outside of the almost 40 resorts, and the nation's capital, only nine islands are inhabited with a population of around 9,000, mainly on Kashidhu in the far north and Guraidhoo in the south. The best fishing is reputedly near Dhiffushi.

Ari—I

Includes Rasdhu and Toddu, two tiny atolls north of Ari, the main atoll. The capital is Mahibadu on the eastern side of the atoll, which has a total population of nearly 8,000. The coral used in Malé is quarried mainly from Fenfushi and Maamigili in the south. Toddu is famed for its watermelons.

Felidhu—J

The most sparsely inhabited atoll of them all, with only 1,500 people on five islands—and obviously destined to become a big tourist area. It has great diving sites like Shark Point, and an unspoilt fishing village at Mundu.

Mulaku—K

Nine islands with about 3,000 people. The capital is Muli, although the biggest island is Dhiggaru. No agriculture at all in this atoll.

North Nilandhe—L
This tiny atoll has only five inhabited isands and just 2,000 souls. Heyerdahl raved about the wonders of the capital, Nilandhu, which seem to be more conjectural than based on actual evidence. The fishing is not so good but it is famous for the tutles that beach on Darabudu during the southwest monsoon period between April and October.

South Nilandhe—M
Eight inhabited islands 150 kilometres (93 miles) south of Malé. The capital, Kudahuvadu, another site praised by Heyerdahl, has a mosque with the finest fingerprint masonry anywhere in the world. The population of 3,000 includes skilled goldsmiths on Rimbadu and Huludeli.

Kolhumadulu—N
One of the very best atolls for fishing, especially near Villifushi, Guraidu and Timarafushi. The capital is Veymandu, and the total population of about 7,000 are spread over 13 islands. More than 50 others are uninhabited.

Hadhdhunmathi—O
The atoll that has it all—good fishing, extensive Buddhist remains, and over 1,000 acres under cultivation. Twelve populated islands with 7,000 people, 75 other islands empty. The capital is Hitadu, though Gamu is bigger. Relics include the mystery dome at Isdu. There's a small airfield on Kadhu

North Huvadu—P
The first atoll south of the 60-mile-wide One and Half Degree Channel. Ten inhabited islands amongst 83 empty ones. The capital is Villingili, population 500.

South Huvadu—Q
This atoll, 340 kilometres (211 miles) south of Malé, has 154 empty islands and only ten populated ones, though with 9,000 inhabitants. Strangely, the usual Maldivian gender balance is reversed here, with women outnumbering men. The biggest island is Tinadu which has very good fishing, its own dialect—very different from northern speech—and a history of separatism that saw it burnt down during the last big revolt in 1962, after which it was empty for four years. Gaddu and Fiyori produce beautiful *tundu kuna* mats using local reeds.

Foammulaku—R

A single-island atoll, population 4,000, with the best soil in the Maldives, and two freshwater lakes. Taro is cultivated here in special pits, and mangoes. On the other hand, it has a treacherous reef, an angry sea and poor fishing. However, the people look bigger and healthier than elsewhere; it must be the fruit. There is no safe anchorage, but the island attracts visitors thanks to the plane connection with Addu.

Addu—S

The southernmost atoll in the Maldives and almost 500 kilometres (310 miles) from Malé, Addu has a very well protected harbour lagoon only accessible through four entrances, and is surrounded by barrier reefs. The population is high, around 14,000. The fishing is no good and atoll life is dominated by the old RAF base on Gan, that now has two garment factories and a government-run guesthouse at which no sensible tourist would wish to stay. The old Koagannu cemetery on Meedu is said to be historically significant.

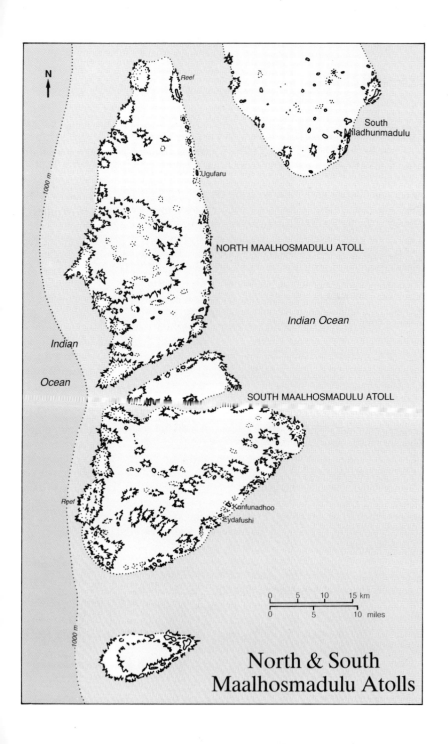

N

Reef

South
Miladhunmadulu

Ugufaru

NORTH MAALHOSMADULU ATOLL

Indian Ocean

1000 m

Indian

Ocean

SOUTH MAALHOSMADULU ATOLL

Reef

Kunfunadhoo
Eydafushi

| 0 | 5 | 10 | 15 km |

| 0 | | 5 | 10 miles |

1000 m

North & South
Maalhosmadulu Atolls

Other Resorts

North Malé Atoll
Club Med Farukolhufushi

From a distance, Club Med looks like a cluster of *dhoni* sails emerging from the palm trees; close-up, the distinctive architecture appears rather frayed around the edges and in need of an overhaul. During the swinging 1970s Club Med was nicknamed 'Club Nature' after its nude sunbathers, who were only outlawed in the Maldives in 1979. Despite Club Med's 'swinging singles' reputation, the unattached are not really encouraged to come here; the management prefers to highlight family entertainment. A lot of money has been spent on renovation—$6 million back in 1985—but the atmosphere remains rather tacky and geared towards package groups. The second largest resort in the Maldives, Club Med does not allow day-visitors or occasional overnight stays. Its 55 European staff rotate every six months, in stark contrast to smaller, family-run resorts. The Japanese like it because of its 'theme' approach.

The 152 triple nonairconditioned rooms are grouped into 19 blocks of apartments; the design is functional and spartan, with fluorescent tubes and no effort to preserve privacy. Buffet meals are served in a large cabana-style, open-air hangar and feature Japanese, Italian, Maldivian, and other Asian dishes. The Club Med style is reinforced by the sight of open-air aerobics instruction by well-built women in skimpy bathing suits for a crowd of overweight Europeans. Not chic.

The main attraction for many is the resort's diving school, which with nine instructors is the largest in the Maldives (known disdainfully in other resorts as a 'diving factory'). Beginners' courses run daily for four to five days. They are all CMAS, not PADI or NAUI, and are well organized. There are about ten good diving spots within an hour's boat ride; group excursions are kept to a maximum of six divers. The school insists on a compulsory medical check-up and has good emergency facilities, including a resident diving doctor. The decompression chamber here is the only one in the Maldives. Video recording equipment is available for hire.

The resort operates the 'bead money' system used by Club Med worldwide. There is an efficient reservation and transport office; nightclub and bar with set meals; boutique and crafts centre. Pleasure trips are available to Thulagiri, Himafushi, and Malé, with round trip prices $26 (adult), $13 (child). Other activities include snorkelling (courses available), picnics, aerobics, yoga, a water gym, Club Med tournaments, sailing, and windsurfing (the large, shallow reef is good for windsurfing)

Price: Peak season s/d $127/220, low season s/d $60/70. Inclusive of
              three buffet meals, all activities and one dive daily.

Transfer: Two kilometres (one mile) from the airport, about 15 minutes
                  by *dhoni*, $10 one-way.
Booking: Tel. 34-3021, 3749, 4552; fax. 34-2415; tlx. 66057
                  MEDMALD MF.

Lankanfinolhu

A mid-range resort with 50 cottage units on a secluded island with a small but
sandy lagoon, Lankanfinolhu is the sort of place that looks unexceptional when
you've seen a number of the resorts, though to the first-timer in need of some
sun it still looks pretty close to heaven. Good diving location.

Price: Peak season, full board, s/d $65/75; low season
                  ten percent less.
Transfer: Ten kilometres (six miles) from the airport, $20.
Booking: Tel. 34-4576, 4582, 3597. Or via local agent,
                  31 Chandani Magu. Tel. 32-3186, 2754; fax. 32-2754;
                  tlx. 66088 LANFIN MF.

Hudhuveli

Adjacent to Bandos, Hudhuveli is run by the same agency in Malé. Named after
its beautiful stretch of white sand, this is a much quieter resort with simple
beachcombing-style accomodation, ideal for honeymooners. There are 44
thatched and rather spartan cottages, though they do have fresh water in the
rooms and 24-hour room service. The resort appeals mainly to British and
German tourists. The diving school is run by two Austrians, and is highly rated
by the Italian cruise yacht skippers, diving instructors, and expatriates in Malé.
Windsurfing conditions are ideal inside the large lagoon and a free boat goes to
the outer reef twice a day for snorkelling. The bar has an adjoining disco in the
evenings. It is said to be possible to make visits to Himmafushi fishing village.

Price: Peak season s/d $65/75; low season s/d $50/68.
Transfer: 14 kilometres (nine miles) from the airport, about
                  50 minutes by *dhoni*, $20
Booking: Tel. 34-3396, 3982-3; fax. 34-3849; tlx. 77035 HUDVELI
                  MF. Or via Deens Orchid Agency, H. Jareeza, Marine Drive.
                  Tel. 32-3779, 2844; fax. 32-3877; tlx. 77061 ORCHID MF.

Leisure Island: Kanuhura—Tari

The 24 airconditioned rooms in this petite resort are grouped in a series of two-
storeyed, whitewashed concrete cottages, and are reserved exclusively for
Italians. The beach is a bit disappointing, especially if you've come all the way
from Europe lured by pictures of sun-drenched sands and drooping palm trees,
but it tries to compensate for this lack with top-flight food in the restaurants, and
amenities like tennis courts, a disco, and an intimate atmosphere.

Price: Peak season, full board, s/d $149/166.
Transfer: 16 kilometres (ten miles) from the airport, $23 return
                by *dhoni*.
Booking: Tel. 34-2881, 3950; fax. 34-4650; tlx. 66119 TARI MF.
                Or via agent Treasure Island Enterprises, 8 Marine Drive.
                Tel. 32-2165, 2537, 3745; fax. 32-2798; tlx. 77071 TIEL
                HQMF.

Little Hura

A lower-to mid-range resort, Little Hura's 38 cottages are grouped in the middle
of the island so that visitors have a choice between the two beaches on opposite
sides. Visitors to Little Hura rate its friendly atmosphere as one of the main
attractions. A full range of watersports and amenities are offered. One nice touch
is the short walk across tidal sands that leads you to a deserted islet, confusingly
called Hura.

Price: Peak season, full board, s/d $73/108; low season s/d $47/73.
Transfer: 16 kilometres (ten miles) from the airport, $20.
Booking: Tel. & fax. 34-4231. Or via agent Hotel Alia, Haveeree
                Higun. Tel. 32-2080, 3445, 2935; tlx. 77032 HOTALIA MF.

Kanifinolhu

Kanifinolhi is just under one kilometre (half a mile) long and 178 metres (196
yards) wide. Its plentiful vegetation makes it one of the more physically attractive resorts, and its white sandy beaches and the extended lagoon make it
perfect for water sports at any time of the year. The island is fringed by a
beautiful reef where snorkelling reveals an endless variety of fish, especially
at the northern end. Boat trips to the reef run every morning and afternoon.

The resort combines traditional with modern architecture and is quite
spartan. It is popular with younger visitors, especially Swedes, Japanese, and
those from Hong Kong. Visitors tend to rate it for the atmosphere, which is
young and fun. There are 13 bungalows served by 130 staff including 13
foreigners. The 130 rooms are very modern—high ceilings and nicely landscaped, giving a fresh and modern feel. Hot and cold desalinated water is on tap;
all rooms have refrigerators, and the deluxe ones are airconditioned. The good
facilities available include boat rental, bank, post office, disco, shops, and a
travel agency. The restaurant serves Asian and western food.

Club EuroDivers under Jose Valverde operates the diving school with four
instructors, including a Swede and a German, who offer all PADI courses up to
Divemaster. Beginner's course, five dives without boat fees, $138; Open Water,
nine dives, $230; Advanced Open Water, five dives, $150; 25 Logbook Dives,
$635; Assistant Instructor, 25 dives, $650. Full equipment hire is $175, tank and
weights only $140; single dives $23, six days, no limit, $204. Other facilities

include Hobi-cats, parasailing, windsurfing, water-skiing, tennis, table tennis, badminton and billiards. Excellent snorkelling from *dhonis* with a free boat to the reef twice a day.

Price:	Singles, full board $75-100; doubles $85-111; triples $133, deluxe only.
Transfer:	19 kilometres (12 miles) from the airport, $25 return by *dhoni*.
Booking:	Tel. 34-3152; fax. 34-4859; tlx. 77096 EUROKAN MF. Or via agent Cyprea Hotels & Travel, 25 Marine Drive. Tel. 32-5367, 2451; fax. 32-3523; tlx. 66026 CYPREA MF.

Lhohifushi

Opened a decade ago in the vanguard of the tourist boom, Lhohifushi appeals mainly to German, English and Swiss package tourists in search of an economical paradise. The 60 basic thatched huts are simply furnished in local materials with ceiling fans but without fresh or hot water. The island has a laid-back, slightly hippie atmosphere right down to the hammocks in the trees. Currently it's probably the cheapest resort with very limited menus, but that will change soon. The Maldivian government virtually forces resort owners to improve facilities and upgrading plans include a Chinese restaurant, two coffee shops, and freshwater supplies from two desalinization plants. This should be ready by mid-1992.

The diving school is run by two Germans and a Swiss, and offers PADI courses up to Advanced Open Water and Rescue Standard. One week unlimited diving $175; ten dives $240; Open Water nine-lesson course $230; Advanced Open Water five-lesson course $150; Rescue three-lesson course $150. Good coral reef for snorkelling and diving. One week unlimited windsurfing $120. Weekly excursions to Meerufenfushi, Asdu, Tulusdu, and the fishing village at Dhiffushi.

Price:	Peak season, full board; s/d $46/68; low season s/d $40/60.
Transfer:	17 kilometres (11 miles) from the airport.
Booking:	Tel. & fax 34-3451. Or via agent Altaf Enterprises, 8 Majeedi Bazaar, Malé 20-02. Tel. 32-3378; fax 32-34 tlx 66047 ALTAF MF.

Gasfinolhu

Small-scale resort of 60 beds in 20 cabana-style huts, ten-year-old Gasfinolhu aims to be an exclusive resort. Its name translates as 'tree on a sandbank'. Closed for renovations at time of writing but is scheduled to reopen July 1991.

Transfer:	20 kilometres (13 miles) from the airport.

The Greenhouse Effect

Climatic cycles and change are a normal feature of the earth's atmosphere, but over the last two centuries natural change has been overshadowed by man-made change. The increased burning of fossil fuels and release of carbon dioxide into the air is altering the make-up of the atmosphere and raising its temperature. The United Nations Intergovernmental Panel on Climate Change reported recently that if nothing is done to change the way we live, by the end of the next century the world could be 2.5° C (4.5°F) warmer and the sea level 0.75 metres (2.5 feet) higher, differences that could signify the Maldives becoming the first civilization since Atlantis to simply disappear beneath the waves.

There are several reasons why this prediction may not come true, and a few good ones why the Maldivians are worried that it will. The sea level may rise because of the melting of the polar ice-caps and the thermal expansion of the oceans as they heat up, both changes that would follow the actual warming of the atmosphere. The main problem for the coral reefs of the Maldives would be that the water temperature could rise too high for the corals to survive.

Coral can live in seawater temperatures of 16–36°C (61–97°F) but for optimum growth the range is 23–25°C (73–77°F). Average annual water temperatures in the Maldives are 25–29°C (77–84°F), so the waters here are already around the upper limit for active reef-building. If sea temperatures were to increase very gradually, no doubt the corals could evolve and adapt to cope with the change. But any sudden rise in temperature (and an average increase of even 1°C over 100 years is quite dramatic in evolutionary terms) could be bad news for the Maldivian reefs.

Other climatic changes could also effect the reefs' survival. Increased cloud cover and rainfall might decrease the ability of the symbiotic algae within the coral to photosynthesize food and oxygen, which in turn would effect the rate of growth of the reef. And the Indian Ocean already has a low concentration of dissolved oxygen. Furthermore, it is losing more water by evaporation than is replenished by rain, so is gradually becoming more saline. The salinity level, like temperature, is quite critical for coral growth and only a narrow range can be tolerated.

The whole question of climatic change is actually very complex, and the possible effects are hard to predict. To make matters even more complicated, not all scientists are convinced that the world is facing a catastrophic global warming. They are in a minority, but their arguments are well-reasoned and sincerely held.

One problem that the Maldives may face—coastal flooding—is not necessarily caused by long-term variation of the sea-level but the combination of high tides, storms and wave action. Three tidal waves in 18 months in the mid-1980s forced many islanders to leave their homes and turned Malé into a temporary lake. In a country where the average altitude is 1.5 metres (five feet) above sea level, building defences is going to be important. Natural reef defences will have to be strengthened, water and food supplies diversified, and building standards adapted. Waves in the Maldives are generally light—three-metre (ten feet) swells are exceptional—so storm defences are not well established. What is more, long narrow islands are the least amenable to engineering protection, which is a last resort anyway. As President Gayoom put it at the Small States Conference on Sea Level Rise in Malé, in November 1989, 'no realistic solutions to our problems have yet been identified' adding that he did not want Maldivians to become environmental refugees.

One area of uncertainty concerns the sea level itself. The net trend in the Pacific and Indian Oceans in the last 3,000 years has been a slight fall in sea level, a fact borne out by several studies over the last 50 years. The sea level today is close to its level during the last interglacial period, about one metre (3.3 feet) higher than during an Ice Age when water is incorporated into the polar ice sheets. Indeed, the

last interglacial, 120,000 years ago, may have been slightly warmer than now with a higher sea level. The latest predictions suggest a 3.7–5.8 millimetre (0.14–0.23 inches) annual rise with guesstimates of around 30–40 centimetres (11.8–15.7 inches) by the year 2050; many estimates are higher some lower. Underlying this is the fact that no one is sure exactly how reef islands are actually built, or what their growth rates are. There is some evidence from islands in the Pacific that coral can catch up after a period of glaciation and subsequent sea level rise. For now it looks a safe bet though to say that although the next 50 years may be OK the world could be facing more serious problems in a century from now.

Meerufenfushi

One of North Malé atoll's largest islands—some 28 hectares (70 acres) in size—and the most easterly resort, Meerufenfushi takes three-quarters of an hour to walk around and is very beautiful. The name means 'sweetwater island', a bit of a misnomer, but it does have a beautiful wide lagoon. There is presently some speculation over whether this idyllic retreat may become a suburb of Malé over the next few years, despite its easterly location. Its 174 beds are popular with large groups, mainly Swedish, German, and British.

The bungalows are laid out in three different sections so that all the rooms have private verandas. The two restaurants' Maldivian chef serves European and Chinese food with occasional barbecues and wonderful lobster. The Sail and Surf School has three instructors who run PADI courses, and the big lagoon is ideal for water sports and snorkelling. Disco and all other amenities.

Price: Peak season, half-full board, single $40-45, double $50-60, triple $65-75.

Transfer: Three hours by boat, or 45 minutes by speedboat. $25 return trip.

Booking: Tel. & fax. 34-3157; tlx. 77002 Champa MF. Or via agent Voyages Maldives. Tel. 32-2430, 2475, 2019; tlx. 66063 VOYAGES MF.

Asdhu

A tiny, idyllic island run by Maldivian entrepreneur, Ahmed Ismail, who also runs the Nasandhura Palace Hotel in Malé. Asdhu is refreshingly simple with an unpretentious style yet high-quality management, and is very popular with Italians who appreciate its intimacy, small-scale charms, and excellent diving school. The 60-bed resort is run as a tight ship. The staff are all Maldivian, apart from a Sri Lankan cook, and they all double up on activities and jobs. There are 30 whitewashed cottages, all immaculately kept and very private with slatted wooden shutters and parquet floors. One lovely Maldivian feature is the woven coir net blinds which open to the sea and sky so you can hear the sound of the waves. Good selection of wines, cocktails, and food in the restaurant.

The diving school has three instructors and keeps its teacher/pupil ratio as low as one to three. The chief instructor, Fabio Valenti, has been in Asdhu for four years and has mapped out 27 dive sites within a half-hour *dhoni*-ride, including one place where you can watch sleeping white sharks. PADI courses are offered in German, Italian, and English. Single dives $35 per dive. Introductory Course $120; Open Water $200. Water-skiing $15 for ten minutes. Also windsurfing and night diving, and excursions to the fishing village on Dhiffushi.

Price: Peak season, full board, s/d $65/75. Off-season 40 percent less.

Transfer: 43 kilometres (27 miles) from the airport, $30 by *dhoni*. Booking Tel. 34-5051. Or via agent Nusandhura Palace Hotel, Marine Drive. Tel. 32-2972; fax. 32-4300; tlx. 66091 POLYCOM MF.

Helengeli

The most northerly of all the resorts in North Malé atoll, Helengeli is small with just 60 beds and basic saltwater showers. Amenities are similarly threadbare, but you can comfort yourself with the thought that you are truly far away from it all. The island has an excellent house reef and isn't visited much in comparison with other resorts' reefs. The diving is very good indeed with lots of big fish.

Price: Peak season full board, s/d $50/65; low season s/d $38/48.

Transfer: 51 kilometres (32 miles) from the airport, $30 by *dhoni*.

Booking: Tel. 34-4615 Or via agent H Zonaria, Marine Drive.
Tel. 32-3339; fax. 32-5150; tlx. 66022 ENGELI MF.

Eriyadhu

This resort has 92 beds beds in 45 bungalows by the water's edge, each with freshwater showers. The rooms are fan-cooled. Eriyadhu is one of the cheaper resorts because of its distance from civilization, but is blessed with a good house reef, a wide beach, and a fine lagoon. Diving is organized by the Swiss Sub-Aqua Club.

Price: Peak season, full board, s/d $55/70; low season s/d $40/55.

Transfer: 39 kilometres (24 miles) from the airport, almost three hours and $35 by *dhoni*.

Booking: Tel. 34-4487. Or via agent AAA Trading. Tel. 32-2417, 4933; fax 32-4943; tlx 66031 ERIYADU MF.

Ziyaaraiyfushi

This mid-range resort on the far western side of the atoll recently doubled in size to 130 beds. The island itself is unspectacular with fewer palm trees than most resorts which makes the bungalows higher than anything else on the island. It makes up for this with a wider range of watersports than most resorts and a well-equipped diving school. Visitors rate its friendly atmosphere to be one of the main attractions of the place. As the cheaper resorts go, Ziyaaraiyfushi represents good value for money.

Price: Peak season, full board, s/d $70/85; low season s/d $50/65.

Transfer: 40 kilometres (25 miles) from the airport, $40 by *dhoni*.

Booking: Tel. 34-3088. Phoenix Travel, Fasmeeru, Marine Drive.
Tel. 32-3181, 3587; fax. 32-5499; tlx. 66107 HORIZON MF.

Makunudhu

The name means 'pestilence island' in Devehi, something which makes the local fishermen chuckle, for the name is at odds with the resort's delightful aspect and its wide and clear lagoon. Swiss-run and very exclusive, Makunudhu caters mainly to stressed-out, security-conscious Europeans in search of soporific luxury. The small, beautiful, and sheltered island hides 31 rooms, all air-conditioned with an IDD telephone and a personal safe deposit. The chef serves delicate dishes *à la nouvelle cuisine,* and among the boutiques there's even room for a beautician. Well-equipped diving school, wide range of watersports amenities, and a good anchorage for passing yachts.

Price:	Peak season, s/d $150/250; low season 50 percent reduction.
Transfer:	34 kilometres (21 miles) from the airport, $75 by speedboat.
Booking:	Tel. 34-3064; fax. 34-5098; tlx. 77059 MAKU MF. Or via agent Makunudu Club, Orchid Magu. Tel. 32-4743; fax. 32-4465; tlx. 77068 GAL MF.

Hembadhu

Thirty bungalows mark this small and remote resort just a stone's throw from Reethi Rah, popular with German groups looking for something a little remote and exclusive. In many ways it has the same feel as Asdhu, carefully looked after and unpretentious, but lacking that slight something that marks it out from the very best.

Price:	Peak season, full board, s/d $50/60; low season s/d $35/45.
Transfer:	39 kilometres (24 miles) from the airport, $30 by *dhoni.*
Booking:	Tel. & fax. 34-3884. Or via agent Journey World, 61 Marine Drive. Tel. & fax. 32-2016; tlx 66084 JEWORLD MF.

Boduhithi

A decade old, Boduhithi has recently been renovated at a cost of $3.5 million as the new Club Vacanze jet-set destination and looks every bit as good as the brochures hint it should be. The 87 thatched bungalows have spacious and elegant rooms furnished with Malaysian and Thai artwork. Some overlook the sea on stilts. Black-tiled bathrooms are finished in wood, the design similiar to the up-market Gangehi resort which used the same architect. Boasts a theatre area, disco, and Maldivian restaurant. One of the best all-round deals in the archipelago.

Price:	Peak season, $140 full board.
Transfer:	29 kilometres (18 miles) from the airport, 3 hours by *dhoni,* 45 minutes by speedboat, $50 one-way.
Booking:	Tel. 34-3193, 3981; fax. 34-2634; tlx. 77044 BODHITI MF. Or via agent Safari Tours, Chandhani Magu; Tel. 32-3524, 3760; fax. 32-2516; tlx. 66030 SAFARI MF.

Kudahithi

An elite adjunct to Boduhithi—boat crossings are free of charge—this eight-year-old resort is supposed to be one of the most exclusive retreats in the Maldives with its six luxurious 'theme' bungalows and just 12 beds. Although well-maintained, it feels a bit self-consciously isolated and certainly does not compare with Cocoa Island, which charges comparable rates. It is also very, very small.

There is an Imelda Marcos feel to the furnishings of the bungalows, each of which follows a different, altogether outrageous design. Popular with business people, it is usually fully booked in peak season. Eighteen staff lurk discreetly to attend to your needs and serve the food produced by an Italian-trained local chef. Activities and amenities are shared with Boduhithi. The 'Arabian Room' comes with a video, a bathroom done out in Italian marble and a bath shaped like a giant plastic clam with brass fittings. The 'Maharani Room' has Indian furniture. Other rooms illustrate a nautical theme with ships' maps and fittings, and a safari room has leopard skin tiles, a plastic crocodile and fake zebra-striped bedspread. The 'Maldivian Room' is the nicest with a bed carved in the shape of a *dhoni*, and a traditional well and open-air toilet in the leafy garden.

Price: Full board, all inclusive, $250.

Transfer: 29 kilometres (18 miles) from the airport, three hours by *dhoni* or one hour by speedboat, $50.

Booking: Tel. & fax. 34-4613. Or via agent Safari Tours, Chandhani Magu Tel. 32-3524, 3760; fax. 32-2516; tlx. 66030 SAFARI MF.

Nakatchafushi

A perfect, teardrop-shaped island with many varieties of colourful birds and insects. The shallow, sandy lagoon and long strip of sand washed clean by the sea make this island especially suitable for families with small children. Nakatchafushi attracts many people who return again and again, mainly British and Germans. Accomodation is in 60 immaculate units, most of which are round with thatched roofs. This pleasantly landscaped 'honeymooners' retreat' has a nice feel with its whitewashed walls and natural furnishings. All rooms are air-conditioned and the ensuite bathrooms have hot and cold desalinated water. An open-sided restaurant and a coffee shop that spills out onto the sands provide perfectly adequate food, while drinks can be enjoyed at the terraced bar on a pleasant wooden deck jutting into the lagoon; the bar also doubles as a disco. The food is mainly continental with specialist buffets and barbecues. Breakfast is the culinary highlight.

The surrounding waters have plenty of coral and fish. Night-fishing and big-game fishing can be arranged. Sports include diving, catamaran-sailing, windsurfing, parasailing, water-skiing, snorkelling, canoeing, volleyball, and table tennis. The resort's two diving instructors, Hans and Christine Hohensinn-Zedelmayer, have lived here for six years and run the Barrakuda International diving school with a local Maldivian divemaster. They offer eight-lesson CMAS and eleven-lesson PADI Open Water courses, spread over four or six days starting twice a week. Around 500-600 people take these courses every year. The resort course costs $160, basic CMAS $230, basic PADI Open Water $320. Advanced courses are $175; six days' diving without limit without equipment $185, with equipment $230; night dives $25. A fleet of boats are available for relaxing excursions to other islands, including Hemadhu and Rasfari just half an hour away. IDD and fax facilities available at reception.

Price: Peak season, full board, s/d $110/120; low season s/d $61/71.

Transfer : 23 kilometres (14 miles) from the airport, $30 by *dhoni*.

Booking: Tel. 34-3846-7, 2665; fax. 34-3848. Or via agent Universal Enterprises, 15 Chandani Road. Tel. 32-3080, 2971, 3512; fax. 32-2678; tlx. 66024 UNIENT MF.

Thulagiri

Originally an offshoot from Club Med, and catering mainly for French people, Thulagiri is entering a new lease of life. The 52 rooms are more basic than Farukolufushi, but much more peaceful, with hot and cold water in every room. Outside amenities now include a 24-hour coffee shop, freshwater swimming pool and a live band once a week. Thulagiri is very popular with divers because of the good diving school, which operates the PADI progression system including Divemaster and Rescue courses. Also catamaran hire, wind-surfing, sailing, and snooker.

Price: Peak and low season, singles or doubles, $90-120.

Transfer: 11 kilometres (seven miles) from the airport, about 45 minutes by *dhoni*, $23 from Club Med.

Booking: Tel. 34-2816, tlx. 66053 THULA MF. Or via agent Deens Orchid Agency, H Jareeza, Marine Drive. Tel. 32-3877; tlx. 77061 ORCHID MF.

Ihuru

Oval-shaped Ihuru recently reopened after renovation with 32 rooms in 16 semi-detached bungalows. It is said to be the most photographed island in the Maldives and is often used as a backdrop for commercials because its scenery captures the essence of Maldivian perfection and isolation. The house reef, known as 'The Wall', is a particularly spectacular diving spot.

Price: Year-round, full board, s/d $65/85.

Transfer: 16 kilometres (ten miles) from the airport, $30 by *dhoni*.

Booking: I Huru Investments Pvt, Malé 20—05. Tel. 32—6720; fax. 32—5933.

Baros

Well-established (it has been operating since 1973) Baros, the 'half-moon shaped island', is popular with German and British package tourists. Its 50 recently renovated rooms stand in ten rows of four facing the sea. The majority of rooms are nonairconditioned and functional with clean tiles and all the standard design features, like dressing table, desalinated water, and a thatched deck for sunning yourself on. The remaining rooms are much more private with thatching, coral, and other traditional Maldivian touches like screw pine matting and lime-based cement. The food is all right but not exceptional. The main restaurant is thatched with a mini fountain in an *all'aperto* arrangement; live music once a week. The bar opposite is furnished in a nautical style with an adjacent coffee shop and boutique.

The well-equipped diving club is run by the Munich-based Sub-Aqua Reisen. PADI diving courses stress careful adjustment to the waters, eleven dives here instead of eight as in most resorts to qualify for the Open Water certificate, in small classes of four. A basic eight-hour windsurfing course costs $120; catamaran hire and water-skiing is also available.

Price: Peak season full board $95/110; low season s/d $50/56

Transfer: Eight kilometres (five miles) from the airport, $20 return by *dhoni*.

Booking: Tel. 34-2672; fax. 34-3497. Or via agent Universal Enterprises, 15 Chandani Road; tel. 32-3080, 2971, 3512; fax. 32-2678; tlx 66024 UNIENT MF.

Bandos

Bandos comes pretty close to what most people might imagine the Maldives to be like, if you do not have superlative expectations. Although beautiful, one side of the island is quite rocky and not as idyllic as many others. It used to be famous for its shark-feeding antics—expert divers would allow a shark to approach and eat fish from their hands and mouths—but this practice is now discouraged for fear of subverting the sharks' docility. Bandos has increased its capacity to 400 beds which are very large by Maldivian standards. It's also used by many airlines as their stopover hotel.

The renovations have made a huge difference to the island's facilities. The Health Club is projected to house a steam bath and a freshwater swimming pool. A sports complex will offer badminton, squash, a jacuzzi, gymnasium and indoor minigolf course. Tennis and aerobics will also be available. A conference hall capable of sitting 250 participants is also on the agenda, aiming to emulate Kurumba. Baby-sitting services cater for the family visitor, IDD and fax for the compulsive communicator.

Of the 125-plus airconditioned rooms, 40 are suites. Only 90 had hot water before renovations began, though desalinized water was available. The rooms are grouped in blocks, some newer, a larger number somewhat spartan, but all the same price. A set-menu main restaurant vies with an alternative serving Chinese food, a 24-hour coffee shop serving Asian and European dishes, and 24-hour room service. The live music in the Sand Bar can be pretty terrible—ersatz Maldivian calypso and troupes performing the *bodu beru* dance on 'Maldivian Nights'.

Outdoor recreation facilities include catamaran sailing—$200 for a week's hire, and a two-day course for $95; the windsurfing basic instruction course is the same price and duration, a private lesson $20; hire of a fun boat for a fortnight $170; and night-fishing. The diving school offers PADI and NAUI courses; a week's unlimited diving from a boat costs $250, exclusive of equipment hire, and a standard dive with full equipment $22.

Excursions to the nearby uninhabited island of Kuda Bandos can be made for snorkelling and picnics. The management have plans over the next few years for a sports complex with indoor badminton and squash courts, a golf course, jacuzzis and a freshwater swimming pool.

Price: Peak season, room-only s/d $68/70; full board s/d $95/155.
               Low season, room only s/d $46/52; full board s/d $65/90.
               Triples are also available.

Transfer: Eight kilometres (five miles) from the airport, about ten
               minutes by speedboat, $20 return.

Booking: Tel. 34-3676, 2527, 3310; fax. 34-3877; tlx. 66050
               BANDOS MF. Or via agent Deens Orchid Agency,
               H. Jareeza, Marine Drive. Tel. 32-3877; tlx. 77061
               ORCHID MF.

Giraavaru

This upmarket resort with 50 bungalows is on an island with little vegetation and few palm trees compared to most. It compensates for this with a very welcoming atmoshpere and some of the best food in the archipelago. Its facilities are also very good and include a small freshwater swimming pool. A full complement of activities, including diving and water-skiing are offered.

Price: Peak season, full board, s/d $100/135; low season
               s/d $75/100.

Transfer: 11 kilometres (seven miles) from the airport, $30 by *dhoni*.

Booking: Tel. 34-4203, 3880-1; fax. 34-4818; tlx. 66059 GIRAVAR
               MF. Or via agent Phoenix Travel, Fasmeeru, Marine Drive
               Tel. 32-3181, 3587; fax. 32-5499; tlx. 66107 HORIZON
               MF.

South Malé Atoll
Bolifushi

A select, mid-priced resort with 32 chalets in two chalet-style blocks nestling in this very small island. All rooms have freshwater showers and are airconditioned. The lagoon is very beautiful and the whole atmosphere of this Sri Lankan-run resort is very service-oriented.

Price: Peak season, full board, s/d $90/125; low season
               s/d $75/85.

Transfer: 14 kilometres (nine miles) from the airport, $25 by *dhoni*.

Booking: Tel. 34-3517; tlx. 66043 IOB MF. Or via agent Phoenix
               Travel, Fasmeeru, Marine Drive. Tel. 32-3181, 3587;
               fax. 32-5499; tlx. 66107. HORIZON MF.

Velassaru—Laguna Beach

This resort has been given a face-lift to make full use of its broad beach of soft
sand that is one of the most beautiful in the archipelago. The 100 rooms are all
airconditioned, arranged either as bungalows or in 28 double-storeyed groups.
Rooms boast a minibar, desalinated water hot and cold, a hair dryer, muzak,
and IDD telephone. The three restaurants serve the usual range of cuisines,
and there's a gym and games room, swimming pool, and tennis court. The well-
equipped dive school run by InterAqua operates beginners' courses, and
windsurfing and parasailing instruction is also available. Excursions in a glass-
bottomed boat and night sailing and fishing can be arranged.

Price:	Peak season, full board, s/d $60/85; low season s/d $50/68.
Transfer:	11 kilometres (seven miles) from the airport, $25 and 30 minutes by *dhoni*.
Booking:	Tel. 34-3041-2. Universal Enterprises, 15 Chandani Road. Tel. 32-3080, 2971, 3512; fax. 32-2678; tlx. 66024 UNIENT MF.

Embudhu Finolhu

Embudhu Finolhu is a mid-priced resort under Australian management, upgraded in 1987. It is a narrow and not especially attractive island at the northern
end of the atoll close to Malé. Its 20 deluxe airconditioned rooms stand on stilts
over the water, each with its own balcony and steps leading down to the water.
The lagoon is sandy and a full range of water sports are offered. A week's
diving twice daily costs $150; a single dive is $25 with equipment. Advertising
material mentions a tethered monkey, which is not everyone's idea of paradise.
Island-hopping tours begin at $20 for the day; catamarans and windsurfers are
for hire, with introductory courses if requested.

Price:	Peak season, full board, s/d $70/90; low season s/d $55/75.
Transfer:	Eight kilometres (five miles) from the airport, 35 minutes by *dhoni*, $20.
Booking:	Tel. 34-4451. Or via agent Shamrock Garage, Chabeylee Magu. Tel. 32-4445; tlx. 66081 DOLPHIN MF.

Embudhu Village

A much bigger resort than neighbouring Embudhu Finolhu, and actually much
more appealing; the island is very pretty with a soft sandy beach and a wide
lagoon. The atmosphere is very welcoming, the sort that works in a resort this
size without seeming insincere. The Village's chief water sports attractions
are the excellent snorkelling available on the house reef and the presence of
the massive channel entrance nearby. This offers chances for widely different
dives to Fusilier Reef to the north and a great drift dive down the channel itself,

known locally as the 'Embudhu Express', where you can float past big fish, rays and sharks.

Price: Peak season, full board, s/d $125/165; low season s/d $90/100.

Transfer: Eight kilometres (five miles) from the airport, 35 minutes by *dhoni*, $20.

Booking: Tel. 34-4776; fax. 34-2673; tlx. 66035 KAIMOO MF.
Or via agent Roanuge, Ameeru Ahmed Magu. Tel. 32-2212.

Dhigufinolhu

The name literally means 'long island', an apt description of this sandbank that's 100 metres (328 feet) long and 60 metres (196 feet) wide, and low on palms and much vegetation. Fifty semidetached bungalows, all airconditioned with the standard minibar, and bath and shower with hot and cold desalinated water. Weekly buffet of local dishes under a German chef, two bars, weekly disco, board games, and late-night coffee shop. Popular with German, British and Japanese tourists who rate its informal atmosphere highly. Locals from neighbouring Guli come over once a week to do the inevitable *bodu beru*.

Price: Peak season, full board; singles, s/d $100/130;
low season $10 less.

Transfer: 19 kilometres (12 miles) from the airport, $35 return by *dhoni*.

Booking: Tel. 34-3599, 3611; fax. 34-2886; tlx. 77006 PALMTRI MF.
Or via agent Universal Enterprises, 15 Chandani Road.
Tel. 32 3080, 2071, 3512; fax, 32-2678; tlx. 66024
UNIENT MF.

Veligandu Huraa

Another newish resort and quite secluded, 'Palm Tree Island' has just 16 rooms, all terraced and under thatched roofs, airconditioned with fans, with ensuite bathrooms with showers and hot and cold desalinated water. The lagoon is wide and clear. The sands are brushed off every night; the resturant is open to the air with a bar over the water. Veligandu Huraa is joined by a 200 metre (220 yards) wooden walkway to the slightly busier island of Dhigufinolhu, so you can share facilities. Or you can walk over to the uninhabited island of Boduhura. Island-hopping and excursions to Malé and nearby boat building villages are arranged, or you can even rent your own sailing *dhoni* for a few hours. The PADI-oriented Aquanaut Diving School is on a separate island nearby called Bushi. The Open Water course is $265; Advanced Open Water $170; Divemaster $400. Water sports facilities are particularly good here. Catamaran hire starts at $150 for ten hours and a beginners' course costs $160; windsurfing is $110 for beginners; two weeks use of a board is $220; waterskiing is $80 per hour.

Prices: Peak season, full board, s/d $130/170; low season
about $10 less.

An Honoured Guest

The one and twentieth of June, wee passed the Equinoctiall toward the North Pole. The second of July in the night, wee were miserably ship-wrackt upon the Bankes of the Maldives. The Inhabitants ledde us all together into a House in the middest of the Ile, where they gave us Fruits, Cocos, and Limons. Then the Governour of the Ile came to us called Ibrahim, who seemed very aged, he could speake some words of Portuguise, by the meanes whereof he asked us many things: after his people rifled us, and tooke away all that wee brought, saying that it did belong unto the King. Having beene in this Lodging the space of a day, they tooke the Master of our Ship with two Marriners, and convayed them to the King fortie leagues distant in the Iland of Male. The King sent his Brother in law with many Souldiers to our ship-wrackt Vessell, to get what they could.

The Kings Brother in law when hee went away, ledde me and two others into the Iland of Paindoüe, where at our first comming the Inhabitants gave us a little food, but when they saw that our companions had money (this money was about five hundred Crownes, which we tooke while wee were in the ship, and the first night we came on Land we buryed in the ground, which they after digged up wanting necessaries, but wee that were in the Ile of Paindoüe had none of it) they tryed by extremitie of famine to make us to give them some also, for they beleeved we had some. By reason of this evill resolution of the Ilanders to give us nothing without money, wee were brought into great miserie. All that wee could doe, was to gather Periwinckles on the Sea shoare to eate, and sometimes to meet with a dead Fish. This extremitie endured a long time, till that the Inhabitants seeing wee had no money, began to have a little more commiseration on us; we offered our service to them, to doe what they would imploy us about.

I went often with them to the neighbouring Ilands to get Cocos, and sometimes on Fishing, and in recompence of my labour they gave me part of the Fish or Cocos. While wee lived thus, I endeavoured my selfe to learne the Language, which my companions despised. The Commander of the Ile seeing mee so studious of the Language, began to esteeme and favour me. Then there came one called Assaul Ocaounas Calogue, a Grand Signior; and because hee saw I could expresse my selfe in their Language, and daily studied to learne it, hee tooke me with him to carrie me to the King.

When wee arrived at Male, hee went presently to the King to render him an account of the Voyage, and among other things failed not to speake of mee to him. In the evening I went into a Court, whither the King was come to see that which was brought from our Ship. I saluted him in the Language, and after the fashion of the Countrey, which pleased him, and gave him occasion to enquire much concerning those things which were brought from the Ship: hee commanded the Signior that brought me, to lodge and entertaine me. The day following, I was busied with relating to the King, the manners and fashions of our people of Europe and of France. Hee made me see the Queenes, who imployed me divers dayes in giving answers to that which they asked me; being curious to understand the Habits, Manners, Marriages, and fashion of our French Dames.

I was about foure or five moneths in good health, and wanted nothing but the exercise of my Religion and my libertie, having all things else to my content. After this, I fell sicke of a hot burning Feaver. There passed not a day but the King and Queenes sent to know how I did, and every houre sent mee delicious viands to eate, and thus I continued a great while. Afterward the King gave me a lodging neere him, and every day rise out of his owne house, and necessarie provisions for my sustenance, hee gave me also a servant and money, and other presents, so that I became somewhat wealthy after the manner of the Countrey.

François Pyrard de Laval,
Hakluytus Posthumus or Purchas His Pilgrimes, *1905*

| Transfer: | 19 kilometres (12 miles) from the airport; 90 minutes by *dhoni* or 45 minutes by speedboat, $35. |
| Booking: | Tel. 34-3882, 3754; fax. 34-2886; tlx. 77006 PALMTRI MF. Or via agent.Universal Enterprises, 15 Chandani Road. Tel. 32-3080, 2971, 3512; fax. 32-2678; tlx. 66024 UNIENT MF. |

Biyadoo

Large at 25 acres and now four years old, this resort is run by the Taj Group, a respected Indian hotel chain. It has 96 airconditioned rooms in six two-storey concrete blocks. The island has luxuriant undergrowth prettily landscaped with bougainvillea a more handsome bigger brother to nearby Villivaru (also Taj-run). There's usually a wide mix of nationalities, mainly German, Austrian and British. Rooms are pleasant without being special—rattan matting, a large double bed, running hot and cold water and mini refrigerator—all overlooking the sea. The restaurant is airconditioned. Other facilities include a video bar, clubhouse, and weekly barbeque, disco, and indoor games. Dinners are a triple buffet of seafood in Maldivian, European, and international styles, as well as great curries. The great plus is the resort's own hydroponic garden where they grow vegetables such as lettuce, tomatoes and cucumbers—quite unique in the Maldives where everything saladlike is flown in. The dive school is shared with Villivaru, see below.

Price:	Peak season, full board, s/d $95/125; low season s/d $68/85.
Transfer:	29 kilometres (18 miles) from the airport, two-and-a-half hours by *dhoni*, $30.
Booking:	Tel. 34-3516, 3978; fax. 3742; tlx. 77003 TAJ MF. Or via agent H Maagala, Ameer Ahmed Magu. Tel. 32-2717.

Villivaru

This tiny 12-acre island beautifully landscaped with palms and shrubs to provide the feeling of a primitive wilderness. It is a shame the beach is not one of the best in the Maldives. The resort has 24 naturally ventilated rooms with ceiling fans, and 36 rooms with airconditioning. Every room has a mini refrigerator and a private veranda that opens onto the beach. The circular bungalows have *satta*-weave interiors, complimentary bathrobes, and a good atmosphere.

There is an airconditioned a la carte restaurant, bar with video screen, club house, weekly barbecue, disco, and indoor games' facilities. There is fresh bread daily; the bar stocks Moet & Chandon and draft Warsteiner beer.

Both of the Taj-run resorts—Villivaru and Biyadoo—share a fully equipped diving school, the Nautico Watersports Centre, offering CMAS, VDTL, and PADI courses. PADI Open Water and Advanced Open Water courses are $300 and $260 respectively. More than half of the guests, most of whom are German, go diving during their stay. Special arrangements can be made for night cruises and night diving, picnics and excursions to other islands, or tours of the reef in a glass-bottomed boat. Daily boat trips (half a day or longer) visit an array of around 40 dive sites making full use of the nine channel openings in the vicinity. Catamaran hire is $140 for ten hours, or $194 for a half day with a guide. Major renovations are planned.

Price: Peak season, full board, s/d $80/120; low season s/d $70/110.

Transfer: 29 kilometres (18 miles) from the airport, two-and-a-half hours by *dhoni*, $30.

Booking: Tel. 34-3598; fax 3742; tlx.77003 TAJ MF. Or via agent H Maagala, Ameer Ahmed Magu. Tel. 32-2717.

Kandooma

A popular resort opened in 1985 and patronized almost exclusively by Germans. Rather plebian, with traces of kitsch like the dolphin murals stencilled on the walls. If you don't have great expectations or are on a tight budget, this is an acceptable low-price option. It has 49 rooms, including 20 individual airconditioned bungalows. The restaurant offers a bland set menu plus Maldivian and German-style buffets. There is a coffee shop and a small seafront bar over the water. Facilities include table tennis, football, and tennis. Water sports include windsurfing at $125 for a course of ten hours, or $175 for two weeks' unlimited use; parasailing, catamaran and dinghy sailing. Extra charges for transfers to the Biyadoo diving centre.

Price: Peak season, full board, s/d $45/55; low season s/d 45/55; low season s/d $35/45.

Transfer: 27 kilometres (17 miles) from the airport, three hours by *dhoni*, $25.

Booking: Tel. 34-4452. Or via agent Shana 2/46 M, Orchid Magu. Tel. 32-3360; tlx. 77073 KANDOO MF.

Bodufinolhu

Better known as 'Fun Island Resort', Bodufinolhu has a long wooden jetty leading to the pier which at night is floodlit to look like a long necklace across the sea. The island is actually very tiny, and is surrounded by a beautiful sandy lagoon, perfect for snorkelling and swimming, and especially safe for children because it remains shallow for a long way out.

Opened in 1980 but upgraded in 1988, the resort's overall look and feel is modern and tasteful. The 88 rooms are in Maldivian-style thatched cottage buildings in blocks of two, three, or four, all simple whitewashed coral and concrete with lots of natural wood. Interiors sport Singaporean furnishings and all rooms have ensuite bathrooms, hot and cold desalinated water, airconditioning, IDD dialing, and a minibar. The resort is very popular with a mix of Italians, Germans, Japanese, and Australians.

There is a lovely well-stocked terraced bar and open air restaurant that looks out over the sea. Food is of a high standard with Asian, Italian, Continental and Maldivian dishes; there is a good list of wines and champagnes, and the coffee shop has a wide à la carte selection.

The well-regarded diving school is run by a friendly Dutch woman called 'Rit' and six instructors, including one Japanese, offering PADI courses. Classes never exceed eight people. The Open Water course is $150, Advanced Open Water $175; two weeks no-limit diving with club tank and weights is $285; a single dive with equipment $25. Day tours roam as far as Embudhu Finolhu, so pretty much the whole of the atoll is fair game if even the giant house reef isn't enough. Nearby is the Guraidhoo Channel and Banana Reef, an excellent spot for hammerhead sharks, manta rays, and whale sharks. Nearby are two uninhabited islands that can be reached at low tide, including a long thin strip of an island measuring only 30 by 800 metres (98 by 262 feet), beautifully shaded and relatively lushly vegetated. Watersports include snorkelling, water-skiing, windsurfing, and fishing. A ten-hour windsurfing course is $115, a private lesson $35; three weeks with a board is $175.

Price: Peak season, full board, s/d $122/132; low season s/d $88/98.

Transfer: 39 kilometres (24 miles) from the airport, 40 minutes by speedboat, $50 return.

Booking: Tel. 4558, 3957/9; fax. 34-3958; tlx. 77099 FUNISLE MF. Or via agent Fun Island Resort, Villa Building, Ibrahim Hassan Didi Magu. Tel. 32-5194-5, 4478; fax. 32-5177.

Filhalhohi

A budget resort with 76 rooms at the far southwestern tip of South Malé atoll, one of the most far-flung spots in the archipelago.

Price: Singles $50–60, doubles $75–85.

Transfer: 45 kilometres (28 miles) from the airport, $30 by *dhoni*.

Booking: Tel. 34-2903; fax. 34-3803; tlx. 66065 LHOHI MF. Or via agent Dhirham Travels & Chandling, Athama Bldg, Famudheyri Magu. Tel. 32-3372; fax. 32-4752; tlx. 66027 DHIRHAM MF.

Rannalhi

This resort is very pretty, with lots of tall palm trees, a wide lagoon, and soft sands; tranquil and natural and not too chic. The over-water coffee shop-cum-bar is now completed, also refurbishment of the main restaurant, and a major restyling is underway of all the cottages which previously were without airconditioning and had only cold showers. There's an excellent dive base but other water sports are not a priority here. One of the better resorts in the archipelago.

Price: Peak season, full board, s/d $60/78; low season s/d $50/65.

Transfer: 37 kilometres (23 miles) from the airport, about 31/2 hours by *dhoni*, $30.

Booking: Tel. 34-2768; fax. 34-2688. Or via agent Jetan Travel Service, 55 Marine Drive. Tel. 32-3323; fax. 4628; tlx. 66086 JETAN MF.

Ari Atoll
Veligandu

Pride of place in Veligandu on Rashu are the eight lovely suites along the water's edge with natural wood furnishings, Maldivian-style open-air bathroom with sunken bathtub and adjacent telephone, and outdoor lights within a frangipani-filled garden. The balcony leads straight down into the sea. There are another 49 cottages, not quite so nice but still high quality, set back within the island. These are mainly twin rooms with some doubles; fresh hot and cold water, minibar, and all airconditioned. The resort attracts 80 percent Italians and 20 percent Swedes.

The atmosphere is very casual at the circular rattan-framed bar with sand underfoot and light cane chairs. The restaurant is similarly casual, and the food is reasonable without being exceptional.

The Crab Diving Centre offers PADI courses up to a maximum of eight pupils per class led by one to three instructors depending on the season. Single dives are $25 inclusive of boat trip; Open Water course $350 inclusive; Advanced Open Water course $300; shark-feeding advertised.

Price: Peak (off peak) full board, single $155 ($75), double $120 ($65).

Transfer: 48 kilometres (30 miles) from aiport. $60 roud trip by *dhoni*. Helicopter link via Rasdhu opening up this season.

Booking: Tel. 960-34-3894; fax. 34-4309. Or via agent Crown Company, 1 Orchid Magu. Tel. 32-2432, 4701; fax. 32-4009; tlx. 66095 CROWN MF.

Kuramathi

Two-and-- half kilometres (one-and-a-half miles) long and just 600 metres (656 yards) wide, Kuramathi on Rasdu is one of a number of islands on which Buddhist relics have been discovered, a reminder of life in these far-flung places more than 1,000 years ago. Today it houses one of the most popular resorts in the southern half of the country (after a major upgrade in 1988). In fact, there are three categories of accommodation here, ranging from the straightforward to the exclusive, yet all sharing many amenities in common.

Laid out in the southeast corner is Kuramathi Village, 122 simple, rooms, either singles or doubles, in round houses or in single-storey blocks. These are not airconditioned and are without hot water. Popular with middle-class Germans, the village has its own diving school; water-skiing costs $7.50 for five minutes, parasailing around the island is $50 for ten minutes.

The second level of luxury is the Blue Lagoon on the 30-metre (33 yards) wide beach. All 50 rooms are airconditioned with their own minibar. Twenty are on stilts with ladders leading down to the water for swimming; double-bedded, tiled, fitted with cane furniture and telephone, they only lack a bath compared to

the remaining 30 described below. This section is only a year or two old and
appeals to the Swiss, Scandinavian, and Hong Kong clientele. The InterAqua
Diving School is a German-Belgian concern.

At the top of the tree is the Kuramathi Cottage Club, 30 separate bungalows
that are spacious and luxurious with their own clubhouse. The Cottage Club is
popular with Italians on a par with Vabbinfaru and Giraavaru—exclusively so
between December and May—and the diving school is, in fact, Italian-run.
The Club scores highly with its excellent food complete with imported pasta
and herbs, a fine lunch and breakfast buffet, and choice of a set-menu dinner or
buffet. The coffee shop has a sun deck with soft sofas, open air and chic. There's
also a boutique. Expect club-style activities; windsurfing is included in the room
in the price, part of which pays for the exclusive jetty. Night-fishing is $20 for
seven hours in a boat off-reef; Hobie-cats and parasailing are also available.

The shared amenities include a sports complex with a freshwater swimming
pool, a gymnasium and a Chinese restaurant. Each section has its own disco, but
the live band has to circulate. Excursions include a full day's sailing at $80 for
a maximum of four people with a barbecue at the end of the trip, and visits to
Rasdhu to see a local school, fishing village, and mosque. Diving spots include
the Madivari coral garden. No-limit diving over six days with full equipment
costs $216.

Price: Kuramathi Village: peak season (off peak), full board, singles

$80 ($40), doubles $85 ($45) 'The Blue Lagoon': on the beach, peak (off peak) singles $66 ($56), doubles $125 ($110); on the water, singles $135 ($125), doubles $90 ($74). Kuramathi Cottage Club; single $110, double $122.

Transfer: 48 kilometres (30 miles) from airport. One-and-a-half hours by speedboat , $30. Helicopter via Rasdhu, $97/

Booking: Tel. 960-34-2456. Or via the agent Universal Enterprises, 15 Chandani Road. Tel. 32-3080, 2971, 3512; fax. 32-2678; tlx. 66024 UNIENT MF.

Velidhu

A large island tucked between two exceptional resorts (Nika and Gangehi) but not itself special at all by comparison. Eighty beds in 16 bungalows. Local staff predominate.

Price: $100 singles, $120 doubles.

Transfer: Six hours by *dhoni* or two hours by speedboat.

Agent: Nusandhura Palace Hotel, Marine Drive. Tel. 32-2972; fax. 32-4300; tlx. 66091 POLYCOM MF.

Madoogali

This resort has 43 rooms, mostly in the form of double cottages, outwardly attacked by the screw pine shoots that make everything look pleasantly, rustically ruined. The clientele are mainly Italians, so there are nine Italian staff. Most rooms are twin-bedded, airconditioned, tiled, and furnished with cane furniture, a bit spartan beneath the A-frame and thatched roofs and there are no telephones. Seven larger 'special' rooms are under construction.

The open-air restaurant serves Italian and Maldivian food with evening waiter service. Breakfast and lunch are buffets. The bar has an interior garden looking out to sea over the small lagoon and a bright pastel colour scheme, a bit kitsch in this setting. Special Doctors Clinic available. Amenities include windsurfing, catamaran-sailing, table tennis, and badminton. The dive school offers PADI , CMAS, and VIT accreditation. Beginners' courses are $280 for PADI and $220 for the others; a single dive is $30.

Price: Peak (off peak) full board, single $330 ($110), double $330 ($140).

Transfer: 78 kilometres (49 miles) from airport. forty minutes by speedboat for $100. Two-and-a-half hours by *dhoni*. $250 round trip by helicopter.

Booking: Tel. 35-0581; tlx. 66126 MADUGAL MF. Or via the agent at 17 Orchid Magu. Tel. 32-2369; tlx. 66075 BLI MF.

Maayafushi

Part of a triangle of resorts run by Treasure Island, an Australian group. Here you use the Club Med-style bead-money system. Set menus in the restaurant offer simple food ('lobster available on request'); cabana-style bar. Sixty twin rooms with a few doubles in blocks of four, plus a handful of honeymoon suites; cold bore-water showers, lino floors and tacky furniture seems to appeal to younger German and Italian package tourists.

Unlimited diving for one week listed as DM330; PADI lessons & CMAS accreditation are given by the resort's five instructors. Nearby is the famous 'Fish Head' reef. Night-diving, windsurfing, catamarans, and water-skiing at $16 for ten minutes, plus trips to nearby, uninhabited Magala island.

Price: Peak season, full board, single $86 ($60), double $101 ($85).
Transfer: 61 kilometres (38 miles) from airport. $60 by *dhoni*.
Booking: Tel. & fax. 960-34-3979. Or via the agent Treasure Island Enterprises, 8 Marine Drive. Tel. 32-2165, 2537, 3745; fax. 32-2798; tlx. 77071 TIEL HQ MF.

Bathala

Bathala is a bit like an Italian version of Club Med—a small resort on a very pretty island with a wide lagoon and soft sandy beach, it has 37 cottages with pointed roofs made of palm branches, each with a private walled garden and shower. A good house reef offers fine diving opportunities for the well-equipped dive school.

Price: Peak season, single-double $149-166.
Transfer: 57 kilometrse (36 miles) from airport. $60 return by boat.
Booking: Jetan Travel Services, 55 Marine Drive. Tel. 32–3323; fax. 32–4628; Tlx. 66086 JETAN MF.

Halaveli

A very attractive resort on a small circular island only 700 metres (765 yards) wide and reserved exclusively for the Italian tour operator, Grande Viaggi. Thirty-one simple bungalows and a circle of white sandy beach. The cook has five years' experience here. Scuba instruction given by three dive leaders; fishing and windsurfing facilities are also available.

Price: Peak season (off peak) $166 ($149) with full facilities inclusive
Transfer: 61 kilometres (38 miles) from airport. $60 return by speedboat.
Booking: Tel. 960-34-3761. Or via agent Akiri, Marine Drive, Malé.

Ellaidu

Sixteen bungalows on a small island means the atmosphere is simple and uncrowded in this mid-range resort that consistently scores high marks with its guests. The island itself is very pretty with a wide, sandy lagoon and a nice sandy beach. Parts of the island are rather waterlogged, but the cottages, many of which are on stilts over the water, make the most of the setting. The management here seems to have got the right formula with a simple, intimate atmosphere and excellent food. The normal range of water sports and scuba opportunities are available.

Price: Peak season (off peak), full board, singles $75 ($60), doubles $90 ($75).

Transfer: 57 kilometres (36 miles) from the airport, $50.

Booking: Tel. & fax. 960-34-4614. Or via agent Safari Tours, Chandhani Magu. Tel. 32-3524, 3760; fax. 32-2516; tlx. 66030 SAFARI MF

Fesdu

A mid-range resort with 45 thatched cottages on
a smallish island. Fesdu offers a friendly atmosphere in this secluded location right in the centre
of the main atoll. Dive rates are the same as at
Kurimathi and the school is run by the same
operators, InterAqua.

Transfer: 64 kilometres (40 miles) from
the airport.

Booking: Tel. 960-34-3741. Or via agent
Universal Enterprises,
15 Chandani Road. Tel. 32-
3080, 2971, 3512; fax. 32-
2678; tlx. 66024 UNIENT MF

Diddhufinolhu—Ari Beach Resort

A high-priced high-class resort that has had
three owners in the last five years. It is at the
southernmost tip of Ari Atoll, the ninety rooms
are quite spartan. A helipad link makes transfers
easy.

Price: Peak season, singles $115, doubles
$120; low season ten percent less.

| Transfer: | 96 kilometres (60 miles) from the airport, three-and-a-half hours by speedboat. |
| Booking: | Tel. 960-34-4409; tlx. 77095 DIDUFIN MF. Or via agent Golden Jet Trade & Travels, 13 Chandhani Magu. Tel. 32-2338. |

Felidhu Atoll
Alimatha

A gem of a resort with 50 rooms in separate huts in the middle of Felidhu Atoll, a sparsely populated group of islands south of South Malé atoll with only two resorts—this one and nearby Dhiggiri. Extremely popular with Italian diving enthusiasts who visit both islands and the surrounding diving areas during the peak season, often with Club Vacanze. Food is an important attraction: the budget for meals is twice as that of large as most other resorts. The management claims a repeat rate of 60 percent after twelve years' operation. The impressive facilities include one of the country's two decompression chambers and an underwater photography school. Windsurfing is also offered.

Price:	S/d $60/85, inclusive rate.
Transfer:	61 kilometres (38 miles) from the airport.
Booking:	Tel. 960-35-0544; fax. 35-0575. Or via agent Safari Tours, Chandhani Magu. Tel. 32-3524, 3760; fax. 32-2516; tlx. 66030 SAFARI MF.

Dhiggiri

This is a very special resort on a small round island, a partner to Alimatha, and Swiss-run under the aegis of its chief client, Manta Reisen. The 35 bungalows nestle in carefully secluded surroundings. The lagoon is particularly pleasant. All the usual amenities and facilities are on offer, including a dive school.

Price:	S/ds $60/85, inclusive rate.
Transfer:	59 kilometres (37 miles) from the airport.
Booking:	Tel. & fax. 960-35-0592. Or via agent Safari Tours, Chandhani Magu. Tel. 32-3524, 3760; fax. 32-2516; tlx. 66030 SAFARI MF.

Faadhippohu Atoll
Kuredhdhu

The northernmost resort in the country, three times the size of the company's other resort at Veligandu, Kuredhdhu has 150 rooms with an open-air feel.However, its resources are not as sophisticated as those found in other

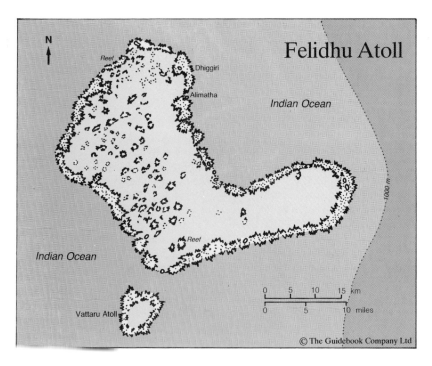

Felidhu Atoll

N

Reef
Dhiggiri
Alimatha

Indian Ocean

1000 m

Indian Ocean

Reef

0   5   10   15 km
0   5   10 miles

Vattaru Atoll

© The Guidebook Company Ltd

resorts. Accommodation includes 15 family bungalows each containing three beds. All rooms have fresh hot and cold water but are without airconditioning, a relic of its former days when it was colloquially known as the 'Camping Resort' by the fraternity of divers that flocked here for the superlative waters. Swedish-managed, with several à la carte restaurants run by a Swedish chef, plus three coffee shops.

Excellent diving centre in a very remote area, and popular with Scandinavians and Germans. Pro-Divers, a Swedish organization, runs PADI courses with eight multilingual instructors from different countries. Three dhonis go beyond the reef daily, so there are good opportunities for experienced divers to make the most of the impressive facilities.

Price: Half board, double room $45, ($35).
Transfer: 128 kilometres (80 miles) to the airport.
Booking: Tel & fax 960-33-0337. Or via the agent Crown Company,
                 1 Orchid Magu. Tel. 32-2432, 4701; fax. 32-4009;
                 tlx. 66095 CROWN MF.

New Resorts

At least 12 new resorts were expected to start operations in the 1990-91 season, all of which are located in Ari Atoll, targetted for future development and the likely site of a lot more resorts once the transport problems are solved. Details available, at the time of going to press, are as follows:

Athurugau Island
C/o Voyages Maldives.
Tel. 35–0508,
32–8605;
fax. 35–0574

Ari Beach Resort
Tel. 35–0512,
32–9354;
fax. 35–0512

Ellaidhoo Resort
C/o Safari Tours. Tel. 35–0614,
32–3524;
fax. 35–4614

Gangehi Resort.
Tel. 35–0505, 32–6687; fax. 35–0506,
32–3364.

Halavelhi Tourist Resort
Tel. 35–0564, 32–2719; fax. 35–0564.

Maayaafushi Tourist Resort
C/o Treasure Island Enterprises Ltd.
Tel. 35–0529, 32–2165; fax. 35–0554,
32–7334.

Thudufushi
C/o Voyages Maldives. Tel. 35–0508;
fax. 35–0515, 32–4435.

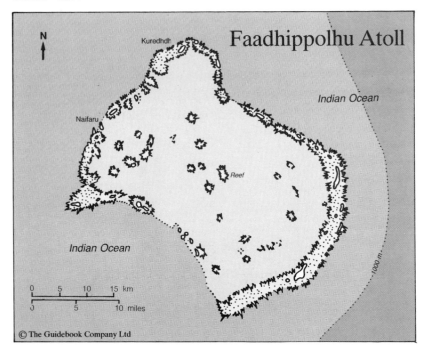

Diving in the Maldives

The Maldvies possesses some of the most spectacular dive spots in the world.
For sheer diversity of the marine fishes and invertebrates it is hard to beat.
They also come big—mantas up to three or four metres (10–13 feet) and plank-
ton-eating whale sharks much larger than that. Snorkellers, of course, can
invesitgate only the upper levels of the water. But scuba divers—'scuba' stands
for 'Self-Contained Underwater Breating Apparatus'—can easily go down to
30 metres (98 feet), the legal limit for recreational dives in the Maldives.
Beyond that depth, even though the water may be clear the dangers of deep
diving increase and render it off-limits to ordinary sport divers.

Decompression dives are illegal in the Maldives This isn't so much of a
problem as it might be as coral does not usually grow much deeper than 20
metres (66 feet). Most fishlife congregates around the coral reefs, so there is
no need to go much deeper, except on a wreck dive. Drift-diving opportunities
abound as ocean currents sweeping across from Indonesia towards Africa pass
the tip of India and Sri Lanka, and surge through the Maldives, funnelled by the
atolls down particular channels. Drift-dives make movement underwater easier
and you do not need to use as much air or energy. The balancing danger is that
unless you watch where you are going you may be swept into coral heads.

Qualifications and Instruction

Scuba diving has become somthing of an industry, with a central core of 200
instructors and more than 60 dive centres catering to the majority of the tourists.
Most resorts have well-equipped dive schools, staffed by qualified instructors.
The best have staff who have worked in the same resort for years, who known
the local reefs like the back of their hand, and who are fluent in two or more
European languages. Courses usually take four to five days to complete, though
some may be shorter. Diving is a potentially hazardous sport that requires care
and attention. As with any sport it is often the most experienced who take
greater risks, and who consequently get caught in a potentially dangerous
situation. Taking shortcuts is not necessarily a clever thing to do—or to be asked
to do so by an instructor—so make demands if he or she wants to rush you.
Most dive shcools operate the PADI certification system which is aimed at
getting sport divers into the water quickly and enjoying themselves. If you want
more training, check out the diving manuals of the BSAC, the most comprehen-
sive of the lot. The main types of diving certification are as follows. All but the
last two are represented in the Maldvies by one school or another.

CMAS—Confederation Mondiale des Activities Subaquatiques (French).
PADI—Professional Association of Diving Instructors (US).
VIT—Verband Internationaler Tauchschulen (German).
Poseidon—Poseidon Nimrod International Diving Club (German).

(Clockwise) Yellow crinoid (featherstar);
coral trout; lionfish on coral; moray eel

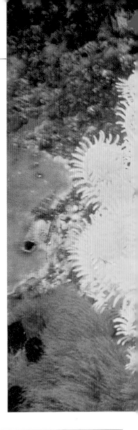

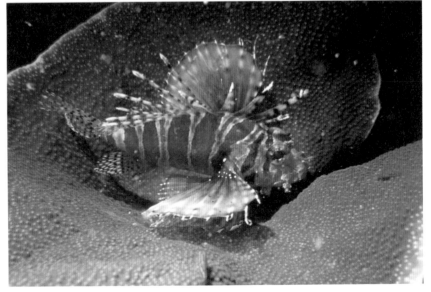

Baracuda—Baracuda International Aquanautic Club (German).
NAUI—National Association of Underwater Instructors (US).
BSAC—British Sub-Aqua Club (UK).

You are cleared to 20 metres (65 feet) if you hold a European (CMAS, VIT, Poseidon) 2-star or PADI Open Water Certificate, and to 30 metres if you are a 3-star or Advanced Open Water diver. Drift diving is being encouraged in some resorts because it is kinder on the reef since the boat above follows the divers by trailing the flow of bubbles rising to the surface, instead of anchoring. (Repeated anchoring in the same area can cause a lot of damage to the coral.) Instructors will also watch out for those not paying attention as hordes of divers bumping into the reef can cause damage too.

The diving instructors will do everying possible to ensure your safety, but in case something does go wrong, the Maldives now has four decompression chambers, in case of emergency: at Club Med and Bandos in North Malé Atoll, at Biyadoo in South Malé Atoll and at Alimatha in Felidhu Atoll.

A week's diving course will cost you about $350 to get the Open Water certification. A beginner's course, by way of an introduction to the sport is $130 for three half-day sessions. Bring a medical certificate to demonstrate your physical preparedness, and check your insurance.

Dive Areas and Conditions

Most diving trips concentrate on North and South Malé Atolls, on Ari Atoll, and to a lesser extent Faadhippolhui and Felidhu Atolls. The water is warm and clear all year-round, though with minor variations locally and seasonally. No wetsuit is necessary, though many people wear a thin suit until acclimatized to Maldive waters. Plankton blooming from mid-April can reduce visibility on the outer reef from about 40 metres (130 feet) down to about 20 metres (65 feet). The richest concentrations of plankton are usually on the eastern side of an atoll, which is where you will find the most fish. The northeast monsoon which arrives in January, brings clearer water to most parts of the atoll. In the clearest conditions you can see up to 70 metres (230 feet) below as you float over the reef edge. Tidal movements are also very important in determining visiblity levels. Incoming tides bring clear water, outgoing ones carry sediment and thus can decrease visibility on the fringing reef and lagoon and reef outlets nearby.

Dangers

Coral reefs are not dangerous places, but there are some points you should bear in mind. Sharks can be seen regularly, though infrequently. Most sharks are not interested in humans, which are not their normal prey. They only do so when provoked or cornered. However, it you see the 'threat display' it is wise to leave the scene. The most common types in the Maldives are the nurse, whitetip, reef blacktip, grey reef, and silvertip sharks. Shark-feeding, an antic which made the Maldives famous, is not encouraged nowadays lest it change the habits of these predators which are, in any case, not always predictable. Barracuda are no danger to humans in clear water but could be a problem in murky waters. The moray eels have very sharp teeth, but the most fearsome-looking are sometimes the gentlest.

Ambush-predators can be a problem for the unwary who stumble onto the reef rather than just look at it. a good reason for diving neutrally bouyant. The scorpion fish has excellent camouflage and is poisonous. Stonefish and stingrays hide under the sand, so shuffle your feet as you move offshore to rouse them. Brightly coloured lionfish floating in mid-water should be avoided. Sea urchin's spines can cause nasty wounds. Fire coral gives a nasty sting, as can some cone shells that deliver a sharp dose of poison to divers who try to collect them.

Some Favourite Dive Spots

In North Malé Atoll, near Girifushi, the **Coral** Garden and the **Blue Lagoon** is home to friendly eels and stingray. The area forms a protective bowl where many varieties of hard coral have formed themselves into a range of fantastic shapes, tall pillars and spreading fronds. Near Himmafushi there is **Rainbow Reef** and **Devil Reef** and near Lankanfinolhu is **Manta Point**, one of the most memorable dive sites in the archipelago, where a seasonal upswelling of plankton-rich water occurs between May and November at the reef's edge where it drops away to 2,000 metres (6,560 feet). Huge mantas come to the cleaning stations here, where they tolerate small groups of divers, and sometimes you can also see the giant whale shark. Manta Point is at its best July through October.

Kurumba has great coral formations at the **Feydhu Caves**. Nearby Bandos has **Shark Point** and **Baracuda Giri,** a diverse coral site with colourful crinoids, pinnacles of soft coral, and—naturally—barracuda. This is a good spot for photographing whitetip reef sharks and reef fishes like clown triggers and angelfish. Baros has a good close dive at **Shallow Point** whilse Giravaru has the **Lion's Head**, now denuded by shark-feeding visitors, but still a formidable outcrop next to the 200-metres (650-feet) deep Vaadhu Channel that runs between North and South Malé atolls. The grey reef sharks here are about two metres (six-feet) long and are not interested in humans.

Near Malé is the **Maldive Victory** wreck dive, where a cargo vessel laden with whisky lies at 35 metres (115 feet) just off the end of the airport runway. It went down in 1981 and is now well encrusted with marine life in its new surroundings. It sits upright on the bottom but is ripped by tidal currents so divers have to fix lines from the dive boat to the masts.

In South Malé Atoll, **Paradise Pass**, which extends both sides of Vaddhu, offers some excellent dive sites including caves, a reef crest falling to around 30 metres (100 feet) and two channels with strong currents where incoming tides whisk you back to the house reef. Neighbouring Embudu has **Fusilier Reef** and the **Embudu Wall** which attracts shoals of small fish which in turn attract skipjacks and yellow fin tuna, and even sailfish and marlin. The **Embudu Express** is the best drift dive in the Maldives, when winter monsoon currents conbined with an incoming tide usher you on a two kilometre (over one mile) ride along the reef wall. Sometimes here you can hear the high-pitched squeaks and clicks of dolphins in the distance.

The dive sites of the Maldvies have never been fully mapped, and the staff at any one resort can only hope to know a few dozen in the vicinity. Nonetheless, as more islands and atolls open up, the number of dive sites—already in the hundreds—will continue to grow. The opportunities for great diving can only get better, if that were possible!

Divehi Glossary

one	ekeh	what did you	
two	dhey	expect?	kiku rani
three	thineh	how much is this?	mi kihaavarakah?
four	hattareh	expensive	vara agu bodu
five	fafeh	cheap	agu heyo
six	hayeh	today	miyadhu
seven	hatheh	yesterday	iyee
eight	asheh	tomorrow	maadhamae
nine	nuvaeh	morning	hendhunu
ten	dhihahe	afternoon	mendhuru fas
		Sunday	aaheeththe
		Monday	hoama
		Tuesday	angaara
hello	assalamu alaekum	Wednesday	budha
I, me	ahareng	Thursday	buraasfathi
you	kaley	Friday	hukura
him, her	eyna	Saturday	honihiru
how are you?	haalu kihine?	atoll	atolu
very well	varah rangakhu	island	dhu (or rah)
thank you	shukuriyiyaa	larger island	fushi
yes	aa	small island	finolhu
no	noon	small	kuda
aiyah!	ekamakuvaa!	big	bodu

round	va	coconut	kurumba
land	bin	vegetables	tharukaree
reef (or submerged coral)	faru	fruit	meva
blue	noo	rice	baiy
dark blue	gadha noo	fish	mas
deep blue	madu noo	turtle	vela
green	moodhu	shark	miaru
shallow	thila	basking shark	faana
turquoise	kula/vilu		nidhanmairu
deep sea	kandu		

Recommended Reading

Battuta, Ibn *Travels in Asia and Africa* (London: Routledge Kegan Paul, 1983)

Bell, H C P *The Maldive Islands: Monograph on the History, Archaeology and Epigraphy* (Colombo: Ceylon Government Press, 1940)

Burgess, C M *The Living Crowries* (New York, London: 1970)

Eibl–Eibesfeldt, I Trans. Gwynne Vevers, *Land of a Thousand Atolls* (London: MacGibbon & Kee, 1965)

Gray, A trans., assisted by H C P Bell *The Voyage of Francois Pyrard de Laval to the East Indies, the Maldives, the Moluccas, and Brazil* (London: Hakluyt Society, 1888)

Hanna, N *BMW Tropical Beach Handbook* (London: Fourth Estate, 1989)

Hass, H *Expedition into the Unknown* (London: Hutchinson, 1965)

Holiday, L *Coral Reefs* (London: Salamander Books, 1989)

Heyerdahl, T *The Maldive Mystery* (London: George Allen & Unwin, 1986)

IUCN Conservation Monitoring Centre *Coral Reefs of the World. Volume 2: Indian Ocean, Red Sea and Gulf* (Cambridge, UK; Gland, Switzerland; Nairobi, Kenya: IUCN/UNEP, 1988)

Maloney, C *People of the Maldives Islands* (London: Longman, 1980)

Moresby, R Indian *Navy Nautical Directions for the Maldive Islands & Chagos Archipelago* (1840)

Webb, PA *Maldives: People and Environment* (Bangkok: Media Transasia, 1988)

Yajima, H., ed. *Islamic History of the Maldives: Hasan Taj-al-Din (Tokyo: Institute for Study of Language and Culture of Africa and Arabia, 1982–4)*

Admiralty maps of the Maldives, can be bought in Alex Perreira's on York Street, Colombo, Sri Lanka. The East Indian Pilot, an Admiralty publication, also has details of the Maldives.

Index